Aromatherapy for
Holistic Therapists

Francesca Gould

Published in 2003 by:
Nelson Thornes Ltd
Delta Place
27 Bath Road
CHELTENHAM
GL53 7TH
United Kingdom

03 04 05 06 07 / 10 9 8 7 6 5

A catalogue record for this book is available from the British Library

ISBN 0 7487 7102 6

Illustrations by Angela Lumley
Page make-up by DC Graphic Design Ltd

Printed and bound in Slovenia by DELO tiskarna by arrangement with Korotan-Ljubljana

Contents

Introduction

In recent years aromatherapy has become extremely popular, as people understand the importance of de-stressing the mind and body. Aromatherapy massage is carried out in clinics, beauty salons, sports centres, on cruise liners, in hotels and even in hospitals, where relaxation is seen as a priority.

This book will be invaluable for anyone embarking on an aromatherapy course. It is specifically written for people taking professional courses such as the VTCT Diploma in Aromatherapy, VTCT Diploma in Advanced Aromatherapy and ITEC Diploma in Aromatherapy qualifications. It is also useful as a reference tool for qualified students who wish to expand their knowledge of aromatherapy.

Over forty essential oils are discussed in detail and you can also colour in each plant to help make learning fun! In Chapter 9 there is a useful reference chart that will help you to choose appropriate essential oils to suit your client's needs. This book is designed to be a workbook and there are tasks and questions to test your knowledge throughout. The multiple-choice questions found at the back of the book will help to test your aromatherapy knowledge and prepare you for final examinations. The answers to the tasks and questions can be found – FREE – at www.saloneducation.co.uk. Good Luck!

Francesca Gould

Acknowlegements

The author would like to thank Heather Mole of VTCT and Melanie Clague of Isle of Man College for reviewing the manuscript and providing helpful comments and recommendations.

The publishers would like to thank the following people for their help in producing this book:

A–Z Botanical Collection Ltd for Figure 3.4 on page 44 and Figure 3.8 on page 51; Corel (NT) for Figure 3.5 on page 47 and Figure 3.7 on page 50; and Mary Evans Picture Library for Figure 1.2 on page 3.

Cover image: Science Photo Library.

Every effort has been made to contact copyright holders and we apologise if anyone has been overlooked.

What is aromatherapy?

Aromatherapy is a holistic treatment involving the use of essential oils extracted from plants to improve physical and emotional well being. It also helps to promote health and vitality by stimulating the body to heal itself and by reducing stress, which is often a cause of many ailments and illnesses.

Essential oils are aromatic, mostly liquid substances extracted from various parts of a plant, such as from petals, barks, twigs, roots, leaves, seeds and resins. There are many ways in which to use essential oils including inhalation, in the bath, compresses and massage. Massage is an excellent way of applying the oils to the body and increases the healing potential of aromatherapy.

History of aromatherapy

Aromatherapy is a holistic treatment, which means that the mind, body and spirit are taken into account to improve the health of an individual. It is by no means a new concept; its roots can be traced back to the early Egyptian people 5,000 years ago.

The Egyptians

The ancient Egyptians are often regarded as the pioneers of aromatherapy. They had a vast knowledge of aromatic plants and used the oils for cosmetic, religious (incense) and medicinal purposes, and to embalm their dead. All of the essential oils have antiseptic properties, which would slow down the decomposition of the body. While unwrapping a

In the times of the Pharaohs poppy extract was used to calm crying children.

3,000-year-old mummy the essential oils of myrrh and cedarwood could still be smelt on the inner bandages.

Figure 1.1 *Theban wall painting showing servants applying essential oils to rich Egyptian women*

The Greeks

The ancient Greeks acquired much of their knowledge about aromatic plants and oils from the Egyptians. They had discovered that the odours of certain flowers were either relaxing or stimulating. They used olive oil to absorb the odour from flower petals or from herbs and used this perfumed oil for both cosmetic and medicinal reasons. Greek soldiers, when going into battle, would take with them an ointment containing myrrh for the treatment of wounds.

Hippocrates was a Greek physician who was regarded as the 'father of medicine'. He used essential oils to rid Athens of plague and also wrote about using plants, such as frankincense, myrrh, roses and opium, for medicinal purposes.

Hippocrates said, 'The way to health is to have an aromatic bath and scented massage every day'.

The Romans

Many Greek doctors were employed in Rome as physicians and shared their knowledge of aromatic oils with the Romans. The Romans not only used the essential oils for medicinal purposes but also to beautify themselves; applying oils before and after bathing and also using them as perfume.

The Middle East

An Arab physician called Avicenna (AD 980–1037) wrote many books on the subject of plants and their effects on the body. He is also thought to have invented the first distillation method for extracting aromatic oils from plants, rose being the first.

Medieval times

From the fourteenth century up to the seventeenth century plague regularly swept Europe with devastating consequences. Bonfires of aromatic woods would be lit in the streets to purify the air. A pomander consisting of an orange stuffed full of cloves would regularly be carried. Doctors often wore a nose-bag containing aromatic herbs to kill germs. Herbs commonly used included cinnamon and cloves.

Figure 1.2 *A medieval doctor wearing a nose-bag*

Aromatherapy in the modern world

Rene-Maurice Gattefosse

Rene-Maurice was a chemist whose family owned a perfumery business. While working in the laboratory he badly burnt his hand and plunged it into a container of lavender essential oil. He found the burn healed quickly without blistering or scarring. He also discovered that many of the essential oils had excellent antiseptic properties and were better than the antiseptics used at that time, which were produced from chemicals and not plant materials.

His first book, written in 1928, was called *Aromatherapie* – the first time this term had been used.

Dr Jean Valnet

During the 1940s and 1950s Dr Valnet was a surgeon in the French army and had used essential oils to treat injured soldiers in the Second World War. He later used them with mentally disturbed patients in psychiatric hospitals. His own aromatherapy book was published in 1964 and, translated, the title meant *The Practice of Aromatherapy.*

Madame Marguerite Maury

Madame Maury was a French biochemist who did not want to advise people to ingest the essential oils. She decided she would like to apply them externally and did some research to find out what effect the oils had on the body mentally and physically. She developed the method of diluting and applying essential oils by massage. She came to England in the 1950s and set up an aromatherapy clinic in London, teaching beauty therapists how to use the oils with massage.

Research and briefly describe the history of aromatherapy in the table below.

History of aromatherapy	Brief description
Egyptians	
Greeks	
Romans	
Middle East	
Medieval times	
Gattefosse	
Dr Valnet	
Madame Maury	

Medicinal drugs

An estimated 40 per cent of all modern pharmaceutical drugs originate from plants or herbs. An example is aspirin, useful for pain relief, which is derived from the bark of the willow tree. It is now artificially made. The anti-cancer medicine Taxol, used to treat ovarian cancer, is derived from the Pacific yew tree.

The drugs called digitoxin and digoxin are derived from the leaves of the foxglove plant (digitalis). They are cardiac stimulants and are used to treat heart problems such as congestive heart failure and irregular heartbeat. These drugs make the heart stronger and more efficient, and therefore improve the blood circulation.

Stress

Today the use of essential oils is becoming increasingly popular as people realise the benefits the oils have in helping to de-stress the mind and body.

Note

It is thought that over 60 per cent of all visits to the doctor are stress-related.

Aromatherapy treatment is excellent for all types of stress-related problems and an understanding of stress and its causes will help you to give your client a holistic treatment. For example, if your client is suffering continual tension headaches, rather than just treating the headache, perhaps the client can be encouraged to take time to relax, make a change of lifestyle in some way such as taking up exercise or adopting a healthier diet, or you could help them develop a positive way of thinking that will alleviate stress and help to prevent the headaches.

Stress and its causes

Stress means different things to different people but generally it is a state we experience when there are demands placed on us and we do not feel we have the ability to cope with them. Sometimes these demands can be stimulating and we cope well, as we feel able to deal with them and in control of the situation. It is generally thought that stress is a bad thing but often it can be positive as it is needed to motivate and make us more effective and challenged.

There are two types of stress: positive stress, such as that experienced by joggers, which they voluntarily place on themselves; or negative stress, that comes, for example, from sitting at a desk piled high with papers with many phones ringing all at once. Other types of negative stress include bereavement, loss of a job, moving house, pregnancy, financial difficulties and break up of relationships. Positive stress could be described as a high, excited tension, when things are going your way in your job so you are achieving something.

Note

'Just for today do not anger, just for today do not worry' – two of the principles of Reiki. Reiki is a Japanese word meaning universal life energy. It is a healing method that draws on the energy that surrounds us to heal both others and ourselves.

Personality traits largely decide which people are most vulnerable to the effects of stress. Competitive, ambitious over-achievers often tend to be stressed. These people can be impatient, hurried and highly conscious of time. People who are easy going and calm are less likely to become stressed. They may often appear patient and relaxed.

Many normally occurring stresses can be dealt with and most people recover from them without any serious ill effect. If stress levels are continually high, however, a person will become anxious and feel overloaded, until eventually exhaustion and burnout occur. When stress becomes excessive it affects every system of the body as well as the mind. Stress is a contributory factor to almost every serious illness. The more stressed you are the more likely it is that you will suffer from both physical and mental problems, which include:

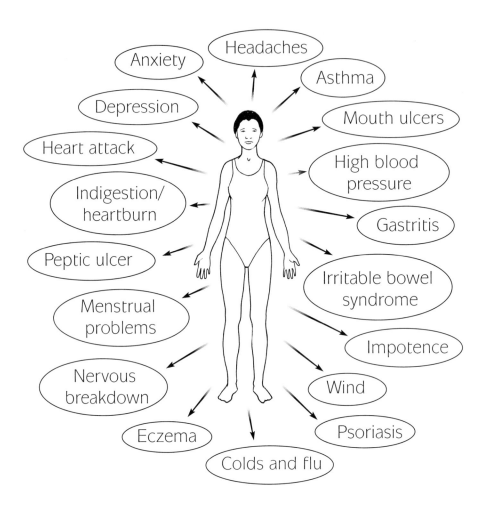

Figure 1.3 *Stress-related health problems*

Men and women often respond differently to stress. Women can tend to become emotional and irritable with headaches, irritable bowel syndrome, anxiety and depression. Men are more likely to suffer high blood pressure.

The following advice can be given to someone suffering from negative stress.

- Become more assertive – learn to say no!

- Turn negative thoughts into positive ones. Negative thoughts never did anyone any good.

- Become more organised and set regular, attainable goals. Tick them off as you achieve them.

- Write things down. This often helps to clear anxieties and fears from the mind.

- Take up a hobby or some sort of activity such as yoga or t'ai chi. These are excellent for relaxation.

- Attend a stress management and relaxation course.

Stress sufferers may overeat, undereat, smoke or drink a lot of alcohol. They should be encouraged to reduce their caffeine and alcohol intake, and also to stop smoking. This will help to limit the amount of toxins entering the body, which will help the body to deal more effectively with the effects of stress. Healthy eating is very important and sufferers should aim to consume a well-balanced diet. Regular exercise such as walking and swimming can also be of great help. Aromatherapy treatments are an excellent way of reducing stress and will help alleviate many of the symptoms associated with stress.

Factors indicating someone
suffering with stress

Useful advice for
stress sufferers

① ....

② ....

③ ....

④ ....

⑤ ....

⑥ ....

① ....

② ....

③ ....

④ ....

⑤ ....

⑥ ....

On the left side of the diagram list some factors that may indicate a client is suffering with stress. On the right list some useful advice that may be given to a stress sufferer.

Write your answers to the questions below, then check against the sample answers on the web site (www.saloneducation.co.uk).

1. What is aromatherapy?

_____

_____

_____

_____

_____

2. Describe three medicinal drugs that are derived from plants.

_____

_____

_____

_____

_____

3. Describe what is meant by the term 'stress'.

_____

_____

_____

_____

_____

4. List some of the illnesses and effects that can be caused by stress.

_____

_____

_____

_____

Essential oils have been used for many years in the perfume, cosmetic and food industries. Much testing has previously been carried out on many of the oils to check for safety and sensitivity. However, it is still important to be cautious when using these powerful substances.

When essential oils are used properly they are very safe substances, but if used incorrectly they can be potentially harmful to the body.

Cautions when using essential oils

- Essential oils are highly inflammable so ensure that they are kept away from fire. If there is a fire involving essential oils, use fire-fighting equipment containing carbon dioxide, foam, dry powder or vaporising liquid. However, you should only operate fire-fighting equipment if trained in its use.

- Essential oils should never be taken orally.

- You should work in a well-ventilated area.

- Spillages should be cleared up immediately and disposed of.

- If the client has sensitive skin or allergies, ensure a skin test is carried out prior to the treatment.

- Ensure a thorough consultation is given to ascertain contra-indications, so that you can be cautious about the essential oils chosen.

- Always keep full and accurate records of the essential oils and amounts used on a client.

In America there are many pine forests and in Australia there are forests with eucalyptus trees. When there are forest fires, because the essential oils contained within the trees are so flammable, the fires spread quickly and small explosions can be seen and heard where the essential oils are bursting into flames.

Storage of oils

It is essential that the oils are properly stored to avoid them becoming rancid (going off) or possible risk of consumption by a child. You will need to consider the following factors.

◆ Ensure that the oils are stored in dark, amber bottles, to protect against ultraviolet light from the sun, which will damage the essential oil molecules. Most oils will be purchased this way.

◆ Store the bottles in a cool, dark, dry place such as a cupboard, as heat can affect the essential oil molecules.

◆ Keep out of the reach of children.

◆ Lids should be tightly closed so the oil does not mix with oxygen and oxidise, and therefore 'go off'.

Most essential oils will last for up to two years. The exceptions are the citrus oils, which will last for about six months. Your nose will help you decide if an oil has gone off!

Hazardous oils

The essential oils in Table 2.1 are based on lists issued by the International Federation of Aromatherapy. They are considered too hazardous to be used in aromatherapy so should be avoided.

Table 2.1 Oils that should not be used at all in aromatherapy

Common name	Botanical name
Bitter almond	*Prunus amygdalis, var. amara*
Aniseed	*Pimpinella anisum*
Arnica	*Arnica montana*
Boldo leaf	*Peumus boldus*
Calamus	*Acorus calamus*
Camphor	*Cinnamomum camphora*
Cassia	*Cinnamomum cassia*
Cinnamon bark	*Cinnamomum zeylanicum*
Costus	*Saussurea lappa*
Elecampane	*Inula helenium*
Bitter fennel	*Foeniculum vulgare*
Horseradish	*Cochlearia armorica*
Jaborandi leaf	*Pilocarpus jaborandi*
Mugwort (armoise)	*Artemisia vulgaris*
Mustard	*Brassica nigra*
Origanum	*Origanum vulgare*
Origanum (Spanish)	*Thymus capitatus*
Pennyroyal (European)	*Mentha pulegium*
Pennyroyal (North American)	*Hedeoma pulegioides*
Dwarf pine	*Pinus pumilio*
Rue	*Ruta graveolens*
Sage	*Salvia officinalis*
Sassafras	*Sassafras albidum*
Sassafras (Brazilian)	*Ocotea cymbarum*
Savin	*Juniperus sabina*
Savory (summer)	*Satureia hortensis*
Savory (winter)	*Satureia montana*
Southernwood	*Artemisia abrotanum*
Tansy	*Tanacetum vulgare*
Thuja (cedarleaf)	*Thuja occidentalis*
Thuja plicata	*Thuja plicata*
Wintergreen	*Gaultheria procumbens*
Wormseed	*Chenopodium anthelminticum*
Wormwood	*Artemisia absinthium*

Decide which bubbles contain a hazardous oil that should not be used at all in aromatherapy and colour these in red.

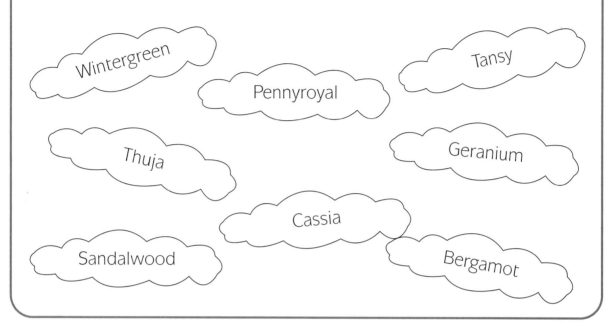

Skin reactions and essential oils

The most common method of applying oils is through massage and occasionally the skin can react to a certain essential oil being used. There are four types of adverse reactions that can occur when essential oils are applied to the skin: sensitisation, irritation, phototoxicity (also known as photosensitisation) and dermal toxicity. Oral toxicity refers to the consumption of toxic oils.

Sensitisation

The first time an essential oil is applied to the skin there may be no adverse reaction but continual use of the same essential oil for prolonged periods may cause sensitivity in anyone, even in those who do not have particularly sensitive skins. The person has become sensitised to the essential oils and may develop symptoms such as itching, sneezing or a more severe reaction such as breathing difficulties. Aromatherapists are most at risk and some will develop dermatitis on the hands through prolonged use of an oil. Once sensitised the body will react to any amount of that oil.

Irritation

This is a process whereby a substance such as an essential oil comes into contact with the skin and causes a reaction such as itching, redness or even a burn. When the substance is removed the area will heal and there will be no more problems unless the substance is reapplied to the skin.

Certain essential oils are known for their tendency to irritate skins so should be avoided or used well diluted. These are clove, oregano and cinnamon leaf.

Note

Undiluted essential oils such as cinnamon bark and peppermint can actually burn the skin with prolonged contact. If irritation occurs apply lots of vegetable oil to dilute the essential oils.

The following oils should be used with caution as they can irritate sensitive skins: rosemary, fennel, pine, peppermint, basil, lemongrass and black pepper.

Allergy testing

Although an allergic reaction to essential oils is unusual, if a client has particularly sensitive skin it may be wise to carry out a skin test.

◆ Mix one drop of the essential oil in a teaspoonful of almond oil.

◆ Rub some of the mixture behind one ear, on the inside of the wrist or at the crook of the arm. These are sensitive areas, which will respond readily if there is a reaction to the essential oil.

- The client should leave the area uncovered and unwashed for at least 24 hours.

- If there is a positive reaction there will be redness, inflammation, itching and the client will probably be scratching the area. If there is no reaction it is safe to use the oil.

- It is important to keep a record of the date and oils tested and state whether there was a positive or negative reaction. Ensure that the client signs the record card.

Phototoxicity (also known as photosensitisation)

Some essential oils can cause skin pigmentation (darkening of the skin) or even burning to occur when applied shortly before exposure to sunlight or ultraviolet light, such as from a sunbed. Bergamot is the most phototoxic oil because it contains chemicals called furocoumarins such as bergaptene, which is thought to interfere with the DNA of the cells responsible for the production of melanin. DNA (deoxyribonucleic acid) is an acid found within the chromosomes of the body's cells. Chromosomes are strings of DNA and carry all the information needed to make an entire human being.

However, it is possible to obtain a furocoumarin-free oil called bergamot FCF, which is therefore non-phototoxic. The following essential oils are also phototoxic: lemon, lime, orange, angelica root and tagetes.

Dermal and oral toxicity

Toxicity means poisoning and at a certain level may be fatal. In aromatherapy the degree of toxicity often depends on how the oils are applied. Therefore toxicity is often classified as either dermal toxicity or oral toxicity.

Dermal toxicity is the degree of toxicity of a substance when it is absorbed through the skin. The greatest hazard is when essential oils are taken orally. The larger the dose the greater the risk of injury.

Note

Remember that even on a cloudy day ultra-violet rays will be penetrating through the clouds.

Acute and chronic toxicity

There are two types of toxicity: acute toxicity and chronic toxicity. Acute toxicity occurs with short-term use of a toxic essential oil, usually involving a single dose that may result in death. When less than a lethal dose of essential oil is used, damage may occur to the liver and/or the kidneys. Chronic toxicity is the long-term use of a toxic essential oil, which may also cause serious health problems.

There are many recorded cases of poisoning from essential oils, all arising from oral ingestion where high amounts were consumed. The following oils have frequently appeared in cases of poisoning:

- camphor
- cinnamon
- citronella
- clove
- eucalyptus
- hyssop
- nutmeg
- parsley
- pennyroyal
- sage
- thuja
- sassafras
- wintergreen
- wormwood
- wormseed.

Write a brief description of each skin reaction in the table below. Include essential oils that have been known to cause reactions.

Skin reaction	Brief description
Sensitisation	
Irritation	
Phototoxicity	
Dermal toxicity	

Overdosage

Applied externally there is little risk if too much essential oil is used, as the body will naturally excrete the oils through sweat, breath and urine. On allergy-prone skin if too much essential oil is used there is a risk of irritation. If too much of a pungent essential oil is used it may cause headaches and nausea for both the therapist and the client so ensure there is good ventilation in the treatment room.

Epilepsy

Certain essential oils are thought to trigger epileptic fits so should not be used on people suffering with epilepsy. These are rosemary, fennel, hyssop and sage.

Note

Insurance companies may not insure you if you carry out aromatherapy massage on a woman in the first trimester of pregnancy.

Using oils during pregnancy

There is debate on the safety of using essential oils during pregnancy. It is not advisable to give an aromatherapy treatment during the first three months of pregnancy (first trimester). In the first trimester there is more risk that the foetus will miscarry.

There are concerns about the use of essential oils during pregnancy for the following reasons:

◆ Some essential oils could cause an abortion.

◆ Some essential oils contain chemicals that affect hormones and so may affect the balance between oestrogen and progesterone.

◆ Some essential oils could damage the development of the foetus.

Therefore, the choice of essential oils after the first three months of pregnancy should be carefully considered and the aromatherapist also needs to remember that after birth the baby will be affected if the mother is breast feeding.

Note

Mandarin is a very safe and popular oil to use after the first trimester.

Table 2.2 Essential oils frequently used after the first trimester

Geranium	Mandarin
Grapefruit	Orange
Ylang-ylang	Bergamot
Petitgrain	Lemon
Frankincense	Sandalwood
Patchouli	Ginger
Chamomile	Pine
Rose otto	Lavender
Neroli	

Emmenagogic oils

Emmenagogic oils bring on menstruation. As a safety precaution during pregnancy, avoid all oils considered to be emmenagogues, which include cedarwood, clary sage, jasmine, juniper, marjoram, myrrh, peppermint and rosemary.

Abortifacient oils

There is no evidence to prove that any essential oils, applied externally, present the risk of being abortifacient. All known cases of abortion or deaths have occurred through use of essential oils orally ingested. The essential oils known to be abortifacient are not in general use by aromatherapists in the UK.

Oestrogen stimulant

Due to their oestrogen stimulant activity it is best to avoid aniseed, fennel and basil.

Advice when treating a pregnant client

◆ Do not treat any pregnant woman with a history of miscarriage, bleeding or any other reason for which she was unable to carry the baby full term. Doctor's advice should be sought.

◆ Use half the recommended dilution you would normally use for adults. This means use only one drop of essential oil to every 5 ml of carrier oil.

Note

The skin becomes more permeable during pregnancy and also more sensitive.

Some aromatherapists will choose to avoid applying essential oils to the skin during pregnancy due to the increased sensitivity of the skin. Others will only use certain oils, which are considered safe after the first three months of pregnancy. Dilution of the oil will be only half the normal recommended dilution for adults. However, you should carry out a skin test prior to the massage.

In each bubble write the name of an essential oil that *can* be used safely after the first trimester.

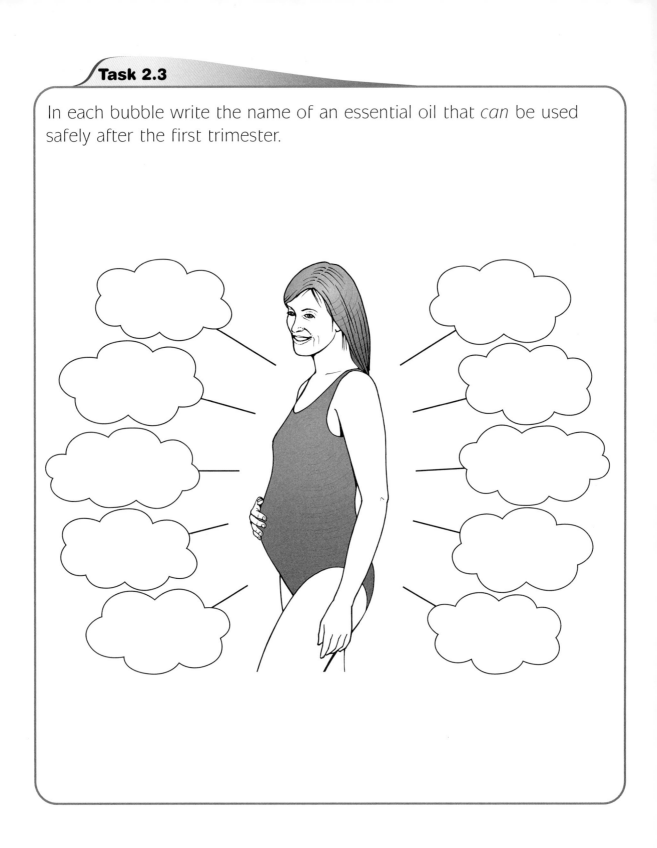

Using oils with children and elderly people

Essential oils can be used safely on children and elderly people, but should be used with caution. Dilutions for children and elderly people are half the recommended dilutions for adults so when carrying out a massage only one drop of essential oil to every 5 ml of carrier oil should be blended. In a bath a maximum of four drops of essential oil in 10 ml of carrier oil can be used.

Note

Ensure that a parent or guardian is present when treating a child.

Accidents with essential oils

- All essential oils, even when diluted, will cause stinging if they get into the eyes. Rinse the eyes with clean, warm water if this happens.

- If neat essential oil is splashed into the eyes then full fat milk is ideal, otherwise use warm water.

- Immediately call for medical assistance if essential oils are accidentally swallowed.

Self-test questions

Write your answers to the questions below, then check against the sample answers on the web site (www.saloneducation.co.uk).

1. List three factors to consider when storing essential oils.

2. Name five precautions to be taken when using essential oils.

3. List five essential oils that are considered too hazardous to use in aromatherapy.

   _____

   _____

   _____

   _____

   _____

4. List four adverse reactions that may occur while using essential oils on the skin.

   _____

   _____

   _____

   _____

5. Describe how and why you would carry out an allergy test.

   _____

   _____

   _____

   _____

   _____

6. Why should certain essential oils be avoided if someone suffers with epilepsy?

   _____

   _____

   _____

   _____

   _____

7. What is meant by overdosage?

    _____

    _____

8. Discuss pregnancy and safety considerations when using essential
    oils.

    _____

    _____

    _____

    _____

    _____

    _____

9. What dilutions of essential oil and carrier oil are recommended for
    children and elderly people?

    _____

    _____

10. What action would you take if a small amount of essential oil
    diluted in vegetable oil accidentally entered the eye?

    _____

    _____

    _____

    _____

Methods of using the oils

As a therapist you will decide the most appropriate and effective method of using the essential oils for your client. There are a variety of ways in which essential oils can be used and these include inhalation, burners, vaporisers, bath, compress, used neat or by massage.

Inhalation

Inhalation of essential oils will help respiratory and emotional conditions. Two drops of essential oils can be placed in a bowl of cold water. This is known as cold inhalation and can be placed a distance from the user to allow a gentle therapeutic application. Steam inhalations are traditionally used to relieve nasal and bronchial congestion or infection.

Treatment plan for steam inhalation

♦ Pour boiling water into a non-metallic bowl.

♦ Position the clients head over the bowl and cover with a towel; this will help prevent the steam and vapours being lost. Ensure that the client's face is far enough away from the boiling water that it does not burn the skin!

♦ Add up to three drops of the chosen essential oil, and ask that the client keeps his or her eyes closed during the treatment.

♦ Ask the client to breathe the vapours slowly three times and then to rest before continuing.

This method can be used up to three times each day for up to three days.

Vaporisers

Essential oils can be warmed so that they evaporate and create an aroma. A popular method is to use a burner.

Burners

A candle can be placed inside a burner and some water and a few drops of essential oil can be placed in a cup-like section at the top of the burner. The heat below will cause the water and oils to evaporate, filling the air with aroma.

Baths

You may recommend that your client use essential oils in their bath. Essential oils do not dissolve in water. Milk is a good medium to use to dilute essential oils before adding them to the bath, but it needs to be full cream milk so that the oil can combine with the fat. Another medium in which essential oils will readily dissolve is alcohol, such as vodka! Four to six drops of the chosen essential oils can be mixed with milk or alcohol and added to the bath.

Compresses

Hot compresses are used where gentle heat is required, such as on a stiff joint. If there is swelling this method should not be used, however.

Cold compresses may be used in cases of swelling to help reduce inflammation.

It is important that the temperature is kept constant during either hot or cold treatment and that the affected area is not over-treated.

Note

Three drops of essential oil can be dabbed on to cotton wool and placed on a radiator. The heat will cause the oil to evaporate and fragrance the room.

Treatment plan for compresses

- Blend the chosen essential oils with alcohol or a carrier oil such as grapeseed oil.

- Add the oil to a bowl of either hot or cold water, depending on the treatment.

- Using either a towel or flannel lift the oil off the surface of the water and apply to the body.

- If applying a warm compress, insulate the area with warm towels to keep the warmth in. If applying a cold compress keep it cool with ice and ensure it is covered well.

- Remove the compress when the client indicates there is a change in temperature.

Neat application of oils

Essential oils should not be applied neat on to the skin without first being mixed with carrier oil. Many essential oils can irritate the skin if applied neat to it. However, there are a few exceptions: lavender can be applied to burns, cuts and insect bites; tea tree to cold sores and spots; and lemon to warts.

Ingestion of oils

Essential oils must not be consumed as they may damage the mucous lining or irritate the stomach and can also be toxic. In France only medical practitioners can prescribe the use of essential oils to be taken orally. These essential oils are usually in capsule form and are made safer for ingestion.

Massage

Note

Remember that when giving an aromatherapy massage the essential oils will also be inhaled.

Massage is an excellent way in which to apply the essential oils. The client will not only receive the therapeutic effects of the essential oils but will benefit greatly from the massage itself. The essential oils are diluted in a carrier oil, sometimes called base oil. The massage is carried out using gentle, relaxing techniques and aids absorption of the essential oils into the body.

Give a brief description of each type of essential oil application method.

Method of application	Brief description
Inhalation	
Burner	
Bath	
Compress	
Neat application	
Ingestion of oils	
Massage (include blending)	

How essential oil molecules enter the body

When essential oils are applied externally, such as during massage, there are two ways in which they may reach the bloodstream: absorption through the air sacs in the lungs and skin absorption.

Absorption via lungs

When inhaled, the essential oil molecules reach the lungs and pass across tiny air sac walls (alveoli) into the surrounding blood capillaries. Clinical trials have shown that small amounts of essential oil constituents can be detected in the blood within minutes of inhalation. The essential oil molecules travel in the bloodstream and are taken around the body to carry out their healing effects. The molecules will later be excreted from the body via sweat, skin, urine, faeces or breathing out.

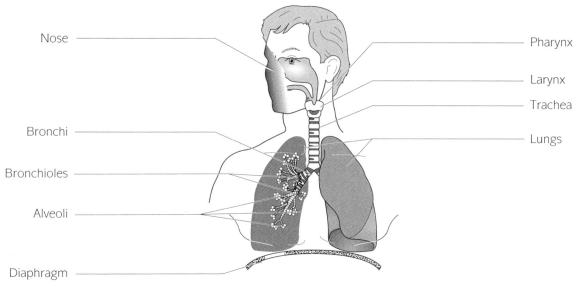

Nose

Bronchi

Bronchioles

Alveoli

Diaphragm

Pharynx

Larynx

Trachea

Lungs

Figure 3.1 *The respiratory system*

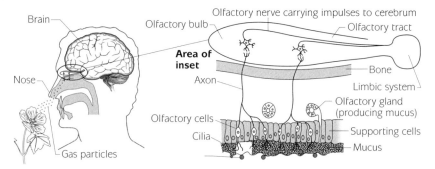

Brain

Nose

Gas particles

Olfactory nerve carrying impulses to cerebrum

Olfactory bulb

Area of inset

Olfactory tract

Axon

Bone

Limbic system

Olfactory gland (producing mucus)

Olfactory cells

Supporting cells

Cilia

Mucus

Figure 3.2 *The olfactory system*

Note

It is vital that your client likes the smell of the blend you make up for him or her.

Substances such as essential oils give off smelly gas particles. These particles are drawn into the nose on inhalation and dissolve into the upper part of the moist mucous membrane of the nasal cavity. The gas particles reach the cilia and stimulate nerve impulses to travel along the axon of the nerve cell, through bones in the skull and to the olfactory bulbs. Nerves from the olfactory bulbs then carry nerve impulses to the brain. The limbic system in the brain interprets the information received from the olfactory bulbs as smell, and we become aware of it. The limbic system also deals with emotions such as pain, anger, pleasure, affection and memory. This is why smells can evoke different emotional responses and can bring back a flood of memories.

Absorption through the skin

Essential oils are easily absorbed into the body when applied to the skin. Tiny molecules of essential oils are thought to pass through hair follicles, sweat glands and through the horny layer of skin (the outer layer) into the deeper layers of the skin. The sebaceous gland is attached to the hair follicle and produces sebum. Sebum is the skin's natural moisturiser and has an affinity with essential oils. The essential oils pass into the bloodstream or are taken up by the lymph and tissue fluid and travel to other parts of the body to exert their healing effects.

Essential oils absorb through the skin at different rates and can take up to ninety minutes to pass into the bloodstream. The skin becomes more receptive to essential oils when warmed, such as during massage.

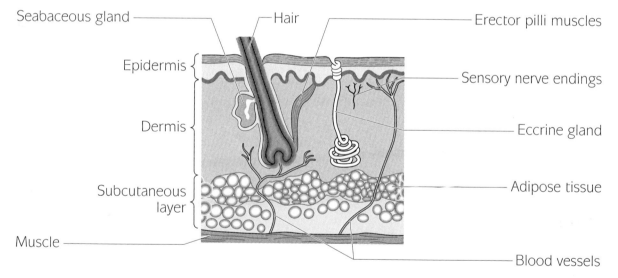

Figure 3.3 *The skin and its structures*

A study that involved using lavender oil diluted in peanut oil and massaging the blend over the stomach area showed chemicals found within lavender to be detected in the blood twenty minutes later. After ninety minutes most of the lavender oil had gone from the blood.

Research is being carried out to find out how the essential oil molecules enter the body and the effects they have on the mind and body. If you need to research this type of information be aware that anecdotal evidence, advertising material and information found on the Internet is not concrete fact. If you carry out research ensure you know the value of that information.

Skin and hair care

A therapist needs to understand the different skin types so that the correct oils can be chosen.

Skin types

Skin types vary from person to person and can be described as being normal, dry, oily, combination, sensitive, dehydrated or mature. Essential oils can be chosen to suit each individual skin type.

Normal

This skin type will look healthy, clear and fresh. It is often seen in children, as external factors and ageing have not yet taken their toll, although the increased activity of hormones at puberty may cause the skin to become greasy. A normal skin type will look neither oily nor dry and will have a fine, even texture. The pores are small and the skin's elasticity is good so it feels soft and firm to the touch. It is usually free of spots and blemishes.

Dry

This skin type is thin, fine and dilated capillaries can often be seen around the cheek and nose areas. The skin will feel and look dry because little sebum is being produced and it is also lacking in moisture. This skin type will often tighten after washing and there may be some dry, flaky patches. There will be no spots or comedomes (blackheads) and no visible open pores. This skin type is prone to premature wrinkling, especially around the eyes, mouth and neck.

Oily

This skin type will look shiny and slightly yellowish (sallow) in colour because of the excess sebum production. Oily skin is coarse, thick and will feel greasy. Enlarged pores can be seen; this is due to the excess production and build up of sebum. Oily skins are more prone to bacterial infections causing spots. Blocked pores often lead to comedomes (blackheads). Oily skin tends to age more slowly as the grease absorbs some of the sun's UV rays and so can protect against its damaging effects. The sebum also helps to keep the skin moisturised and prevents drying.

Note

Acne vulgaris is a skin condition in which there are red, swollen spots and blackheads, found mainly on the face and back. It often affects teenagers and is caused by an overproduction of sebum due to hormone stimulation.

Combination

With this skin type there will be areas of dry, normal and greasy skin. Usually the forehead, nose and chin are greasy and this area is known as the T zone. The areas around the eyes and cheeks are usually dry and perhaps sensitive.

Sensitive

This skin type is often dry, transparent and reddens easily when touched. Dilated capillaries may be present, especially on the cheeks, which gives the face a high red colour, known as couperouse skin. Hereditary factors may be a cause of sensitive skin. Certain substances may easily irritate a sensitive skin so care should be taken when choosing products for this type. If a white skin is sensitive to a product it will show as a reddened area but on black skin it will show up as a darkened area.

Dehydrated

This skin type lacks moisture and so is dehydrated. The causes include illness, medication, too much sun, dieting and working in a dry environment with low humidity, such as an air-conditioned office. Sebum helps to prevent evaporation of water from the skin, so when insufficient sebum is produced, moisture is lost from the skin. The skin feels and looks dry and tight. There may be flaking and fine lines present on the skin. Dilated capillaries are also common with this skin type.

Mature

This skin type is dry as the sebaceous and sweat glands become less active. The skin may be thin and wrinkles will be present. There are usually dilated capillaries, often around the nose and cheek areas. The bone structure can become more prominent as the adipose (fat) and supportive (i.e. collagen) tissues become thinner. Muscle tone is often poor so the contours of the face become slack. Due to the poor blood circulation waste products are removed less quickly so the skin may become puffy and pale in colour. Liver spots may also appear on the face and hands. The cause of this skin type is ageing and altered hormone activity.

Task 3.2

State two factors that would indicate the following skin types:

Skin type	Indications
Dry	
Oily	
Combination	
Sensitive	
Dehydrated	
Mature	

Aromatherapy skin care

Aromatherapy skin care consists of cleanse, tone and moisturise. Various essential oils can be used to treat certain skin types. For more detail on this, see the reference chart in Chapter 9.

Cleansers

Cleansers help to remove dirt, make-up and excess sebum from the face. Essential oils can be added to a pure, unperfumed cleanser. Cold-pressed jojoba oil makes an ideal cleanser and can be used to remove eye make-up. The cleanser can be applied with the fingers and wiped gently away with damp cotton wool pads.

Toners

Toners are used to remove all traces of cleanser and act as a gentle astringent (tighten skin tissues). Flower waters, such as rose water or orange flower water, can be used as toners. Apply the toner to damp cotton wool pads and wipe gently over the skin.

Moisturisers

Moisturising creams consist of water, oil and wax. The oil-based creams can be used as carriers for the essential oils.

Moisturisers are beneficial to the skin for the following reasons:

- They help prevent moisture loss by adding a protective film to the skin.
- They soften the skin so that it feels smooth.
- They help to protect skin against dirt and pollution by acting as a barrier.

Masks

Clay masks contain natural earth ingredients and help to draw out dirt and grime from the skin. The masks are applied to the neck and face in a thin layer. The effects of the mask depend on the ingredients used and how long they stay on the face.

Table 3.1   Clay masks and their benefits

Clay mask	Description
Calamine (pink powder)	Gentle action on the skin, which soothes and calms. Used for sensitive skin.
Magnesium carbonate (white powder)	Gentle action, which tightens the pores, and softens the skin. Can be used for normal to dry skin types. Can be mixed with calamine for dry, sensitive skin.
Kaolin (white powder)	Has a deep cleansing effect and removes impurities from the skin. It improves blood and lymphatic circulations. Useful for congested, oily skin (with spots or blackheads).
Fuller's earth (grey/green powder)	Very deep cleansing and stimulates blood circulation. Not suitable for sensitive skin but ideal for oily, congested skins.

The clay mask is mixed with a suitable lubricant, often flower waters, until it becomes a paste. For dry skin types rose water can be used, witch hazel is used for greasy skin and vegetable oil for sensitive skins. Two drops of essential oils can be added to the mask to benefit a certain skin type.

Note

Be careful to avoid applying the mask too near the eyes.

The mixture is applied to the face and neck with a mask brush (ensure a hair band secures the hair back) and is left on for about ten minutes. To remove the mask use damp sponges or flannels that have been soaked in warm water. Remove the mask gently and do not drag the skin.

State the reasons for using the following skin care products:

Skin care product	Benefits
Cleansers	
Toners	
Moisturisers	
Masks	

Essential oils and the hair

Traditionally chamomile shampoo has been used to enhance blonde hair, sage or rosemary shampoo to enhance dark hair, and carrot to enhance ginger hair. Three drops of chamomile, rosemary, sage or carrot can be added to a mild, unperfumed shampoo.

Note

See Chapter 9 for details of oils that can help dry and greasy hair types.

Blending of essential and carrier oils

Essential oils can be added to creams, lotions and oils. These products can be used to moisturise the skin or to carry out a massage. If possible use pure, unperfumed products and add two drops of essential oil to every 5 ml of the carrier oil, lotion or cream.

Note

Beeswax is used in the making of creams and ointments. Essential oils can be added to the beeswax and are effective in the treatment of skin disorders.

When blending essential oils with carrier oils, a dilution of 2 per cent is usually recommended. To ensure a dilution of 2 per cent you can divide the amount of millilitres of carrier oil you intend to use by half and that will determine how many drops of essential oils you can use. For instance, if you use 20 ml of carrier oil you can use up to ten drops of essential oils. Ensure you measure the amount of both oils in a measuring pot to ensure a safe dilution.

Another popular method of measuring a blend is to measure two drops of essential oil to every 5 ml of carrier oil when blending. An average client will need around 20 ml of carrier oil. A small-framed client may need around 15 ml and a large client around 25 ml of carrier oil.

Up to three essential oils only should be blended together and used for each treatment. A well-balanced blend of essential oils will contain base, middle and top notes, although if you require a stimulating blend use mainly top notes. For a sedating blend use mainly base notes.

Top/middle/base notes

Note

Chapter 5 discusses the oils and states which oils blend well with each other.

In the nineteeth century a Frenchman, Piesse, developed a way of categorising odours according to musical notes in a scale. The practice of arranging essential oils and perfume ingredients into top notes, middles notes and base notes forms the basis of creating a well-balanced perfume and these principles may also be applied to aromatherapy.

A combination of bergamot and sandalwood, for example, can be very fresh and fruity at first, becoming more woody and balsamic later.

Essential oils can be split into groups according to how volatile they are (how quickly they evaporate into the air).

Top notes

- Top notes evaporate into the air most quickly.

- They will hit you first in a blend, so give the first impression of the blend.

- They are the fastest acting on the body.

- They are most stimulating and uplifting to mind and body.

- They are mostly obtained from citrus fruits.

Middle notes

- Middle notes evaporate at a moderate pace.

- They mostly regulate the bodily functions, such as digestion.

- They are mainly obtained from flowers and herbs.

Base notes

- Base notes are slowest to evaporate into the air.

- They act as a fixative, helping to slow down the evaporation of the more volatile essential oils, therefore making their fragrance last longer.

- They sedate and relax the mind and body.

- They are mostly obtained from woods and resins.

Note

A well-balanced blend of essential oils will contain base, middle and top notes.

Note

In perfumery, base notes are used as a fixative to help the fragrance of the perfume last longer.

Synergy

Synergy is the combining of substances to increase their therapeutic effects. For instance, the anti-inflammatory effect of chamomile is increased by the addition of lavender oil.

Synergy

Blending the oils may take into account the notes and aroma of the essential oils. When two or three essential oils blend well together, they enhance each other's properties as their molecules combine to form a synergy. This synergistic blend will have more powerful therapeutic effects than if using only one of the essential oils on its own.

Task 3.4

Give a brief description of each of the notes below.

Notes	Brief description
Top	
Middle	
Base	

Choosing oils to suit your client's needs

Some clients may present you with more than one condition, for example, eczema, pre-menstrual syndrome and symptoms of stress. Obviously you would like to use essential oils that would benefit all the conditions. Below is a cross-reference chart that will help you to select the most suitable oils for this combination of conditions.

Note

Chapter 9 consists of an 'Essential oils and conditions reference chart' to help you decide which oils to choose for each condition presented by a client. With practice you will know instinctively which oils to use for each client.

Table 3.2 Essential oils for different conditions (1)

	Condition 1 **Stress**	Condition 2 **Eczema**	Condition 3 **Pre-menstrual syndrome**
Top note	Clary sage, bergamot, petitgrain	Bergamot, thyme	Clary sage
Middle note	Lavender, melissa, chamomile, geranium, rosewood	Lavender, chamomile, geranium, juniper, carrot seed	Lavender, geranium, chamomile, melissa, marjoram, rosewood
Base note	Ylang-ylang, patchouli	Myrrh, patchouli, rose	Rose, neroli

Essential oils chosen and amount used: clary sage, lavender, patchouli – two drops of each.

Carrier oil chosen and amount used: sweet almond (20 ml).

For a client suffering with symptoms of stress, mild eczema and pre-menstrual tension the following oils can be used:

- Clary sage can be chosen as it will help with stress and pre-menstrual tension.

- Bergamot will help with stress and eczema.

- Patchouli will help with stress and eczema.

- Rose will help with eczema and pre-menstrual tension.

- Lavender, chamomile and geranium will help all the conditions.

Use Chapter 9 to research suitable oils for the conditions listed in the table below. Complete the table and put a circle around the essential oils you would choose to use on this particular client.

Table 3.3 **Essential oils for different conditions (2)**

	Condition 1 Insomnia	Condition 2 Irregular periods	Condition 3 Mature skin
Top note			
Middle note			
Base note			

Carrier oils

It is important that the essential oils are mixed with a carrier oil prior to use if massaging to help disperse the essential oils. The plant oils used as carriers in aromatherapy are referred to as fixed oils because they do not evaporate.

The carrier oil can be used on its own with the essential oils (known as the main carrier) or small amounts of other carrier oils can be mixed with them. Grapeseed and sweet almond oils are excellent to use as main carriers. Other oils, such as jojoba, can be mixed with the carrier oils in small amounts before blending in the essential oils.

The carrier oils should be unrefined, as the refining process means that the oils are extracted at high temperature resulting in nutrients being destroyed. This type of oil is often found on the supermarket shelves. Carrier oils should be cold pressed and preferably free of additives, so look at the product label. Cold pressing involves pressing the nuts, kernels or seeds etc. with a hydraulic press so that the oil is squeezed out with no heating involved. Therefore the oils retain their natural properties.

Mineral oils are not used in aromatherapy as they have poor penetrative qualities and have a tendency to clog the pores of the skin.

Essential oils molecules are small enough to penetrate through the skin and into the bloodstream. The carrier oil molecules tend to be larger so mostly absorb into the upper layers of the skin and do not pass into the bloodstream.

Allergy testing

For some of the carrier oils it is advised to give an allergy test, particularly if the client has sensitive skin.

Note

Allergy testing: place a couple of dabs of carrier oil behind the client's ear using a cotton bud. The oil should be left on for about 24 hours. Often a reaction will show fairly quickly. It is advisable not to use the oil if there is redness, inflammation or itching.

There are many carrier oils used in aromatherapy. These include sweet almond, apricot kernel, avocado, calendula, coconut, evening primrose, grapeseed, jojoba, macadamia, olive, peach kernel, sesame, sunflower and wheatgerm. The remainder of this chapter describes their properties and benefits.

Sweet almond oil

The sweet almond tree is grown in Mediterranean countries and California in North America. Sweet almond oil is extracted from the kernels of nuts belonging to the tree. It is a pale yellow, thick liquid that mixes well with most other carrier oils and essential oils. This popular oil is rich in nutrients, such as unsaturated fatty acids, protein and vitamins A, B, D and E.

Figure 3.4 *Sweet almond tree* (Prunus dulcis)

Uses of sweet almond oil

- Helps muscular tension, pain and stiffness.
- Excellent moisturiser for skin and hair.
- Helps to soothe and reduce inflammation.
- Beneficial for relieving itchiness associated with skin conditions such as eczema and psoriasis.

Sweet almond is a safe oil to use but it is advisable not to use it on someone suffering from a nut allergy.

Apricot kernel oil

The apricot tree is native to China but now grown in many countries including North America and the South of France. The oil is extracted from the apricot nut and is very similar to sweet almond oil but a little more expensive. Sometimes other oils are added such as sweet almond and cherry oil.

Uses of apricot kernel oil

- Moisturising and nourishing for the skin.
- Beneficial in relieving itching associated with dry skin.
- Suitable for sensitive, dry and ageing skin types.

Avocado oil

The avocado tree is grown in many countries especially Spain. The oil is taken from the flesh of the avocado fruit and is green. It is solid at 0°C but liquefies at room temperature.

The oil contains vitamins A, B₁, B₂ and D and many minerals including potassium, phosphorus, magnesium and calcium. It also contains proteins and fats. This oil is quite expensive so is often added to other carrier oils.

Uses of avocado oil

- Excellent moisturiser for the skin.

- Penetrates deeper into the epidermis than most other carrier oils.

- Has skin healing properties and helps reduce inflammation so is useful for conditions such as psoriasis and eczema.

- Helps to prevent premature ageing of the skin.

- When mixing up an aromatherapy blend use 10 per cent of avocado oil. The other 90 per cent of the carrier oil can be made up with an oil such as olive oil.

Note

Crushed avocado pulp left on the face for twenty minutes will cleanse and moisturise the skin.

Calendula oil (also known as pot marigold)

This plant originated from the Mediterranean but is now grown all over the world. It produces bright yellow to orange coloured flowers.

Calendula oil is extracted by a process called maceration. The flowers are chopped up and added to a carrier oil, often olive or sunflower oil. The mixture is shaken for a time and then placed out in the sunshine for several days. The essential oil from the flowers combines with the carrier oil and this macerated mixture is then filtered to remove any of the plant parts that are left. The remaining liquid is known as calendula oil or marigold oil.

Uses of calendula oil

◊ Helpful for dry skin conditions such as eczema.

◊ Useful to help heal cuts and bruises.

Calendula can be mixed with another carrier oil as it is quite expensive.

Coconut

Note

There are two types of marigold; calendula and tagetes. Tagetes is an essential oil from a different plant and is also known as marigold oil.

The palm tree is cultivated in many tropical areas such as Africa and South East Asia. Coconut oil is a cream-coloured oil extracted from the dried flesh of the coconut. The oil is light and has a beautiful aroma. At room temperature coconut oil will be solid but will liquefy when warm. Placing the pot by a radiator or in warm water for a few minutes will liquefy the oil.

Figure 3.5 *Coconut palm* (Cocos nucifera)

Note

Coconut oil is a highly refined oil so many of the nutrients are destroyed during the refining process.

Uses of coconut oil

◊ Softening and moisturising to the skin and hair.

◊ Relieves inflamed skin.

It can be used on its own or mixed with other carrier oils. It may irritate sensitive skin so an allergy test should be given. It is advisable not to use it on someone with a nut allergy.

Evening primrose oil

The evening primrose plant is native to North America but is now common in the Mediterranean, and is also grown in the UK. It is a plant that has yellow coloured flowers. Evening primrose oil is extracted from the seeds of the plant.

Uses of evening primrose oil

- ◆ Useful for dry, scaly skin.
- ◆ Helps wounds to heal.
- ◆ Useful for eczema.
- ◆ Helps to prevent dandruff.

It would be expensive to use this oil only as a carrier. Evening primrose oil can be added to a carrier oil in the proportion of 10 per cent to 90 per cent of a main carrier such as sweet almond.

Grapeseed oil

Grapeseed oil originated in France but is now mainly produced in Spain, Italy and California in North America. The plant is a climbing vine that produces grapes. The seeds of the grape yield an oil of high quality that is almost colourless. The refined oil keeps fairly well.

Uses of grapeseed oil

- ◆ Moisturising to the skin.
- ◆ Useful for clients who do not like oils that are too greasy.

Jojoba (pronounced *ho-ho-ba*) oil

Jojoba is a light yellow, waxy vegetable oil extracted from the crushed seeds of the jojoba shrub. This evergreen shrub grows in deserts and is native to Mexico in South America, and Arizona and California in North America. It is a nutritious oil containing vitamin E, minerals and proteins, which are absorbed into the skin. Unlike many other oils it can be heated to high temperatures and will still retain its nutrients.

At room temperature it is semi-solid due to its waxy consistency but solidifies when put in the fridge. It does not oxidise (mix with oxygen), therefore it keeps very well. It is good for all hair and skin types including oily skins.

Figure 3.6 *The jojobo plant* (Simmondria chinensis)

Uses of jojoba oil

- Good for moisturising the skin and hair.

- Helps to relieve inflammation, so is excellent for acne, eczema, psoriasis and arthritis.

- Beneficial for all types of skin.

- Helps to control the release of sebum so is useful for seborrhoeic skin conditions.

Jojoba is an expensive oil so it is wise to use a small amount and mix it with another carrier oil such as sweet almond. It is generally a safe oil to use.

Macadamia oil

The macadamia tree is native to Australia, and grows in subtropical forests. The tree produces nuts, from which the oil is taken, and creamy white or pink blossoms.

The oil is cold pressed and is available either refined or unrefined. In both cases solvents are not used and the oil retains its natural properties.

Uses of macadamia oil

- Thought to help prevent skin ageing.

- Good for moisturising the skin.

- It has good keeping properties so will last quite a long time before becoming rancid (going off).

Olive oil

Note

When consumed macadamia oil has a mild laxative action.

Olive oil is a yellow/green oil extracted from the flesh of the olive. Olives are fruits grown on trees mainly in the Mediterranean. The oil has a thick consistency and strong odour so is often mixed with a lighter oil such as sweet almond. It is a good source of vitamin E and is useful for dehydrated and inflamed skin. It is an oil commonly used in cooking.

Figure 3.7 *Olive trees* (Olea europaea)

Uses of olive oil

- Helps to moisturise the skin and hair, so prevents dryness.

- Helps to relieve muscular stiffness and pain.

It is preferable to use virgin or extra virgin oil. Olive oil is a safe oil to use on the skin and rarely causes irritation; it is therefore an ideal oil to use on children.

Peach kernel oil

The small peach tree originates from China but the major producers are now California and Texas in North America. The tree produces fruits, peaches, which contain kernels.

The oil is obtained by cold pressing the kernels and is very similar in appearance and chemically to apricot and sweet almond oils.

Uses of peach kernel oil

- Nourishing and moisturising to skin.
- Useful for dry skins and eczema.
- Helps relieve itching, so can be useful for psoriasis.
- Good for sensitive skins.

Sesame oil

The sesame plant originates from the East Indies but is now grown in many countries, especially China, India, Africa and South America. It has long, bell-like, white flowers similar to those of the foxglove. Sesame seeds are extracted from the sesame plant by shaking the dried plant upside down after making an incision in the seedpod. Sesame oil is extracted from sesame seeds. Sesame oil is a thick liquid with a golden/yellow colour and has a slight nutty aroma.

Note

It was the Romans who brought peaches to Europe.

Sesame seeds are rich in vitamin E and minerals such as iron, calcium and phosphorus. The oil has similar properties to olive oil. It has excellent keeping qualities.

Uses of sesame oil

- Helps relieve muscular aches, pains and stiffness.

- Moisturises dry skin and is helpful for eczema and psoriasis.

- It is thought to prevent hair from turning grey!

Sometimes sesame oil may irritate a sensitive skin so an allergy test may need to be given before using it. Olive oil is an excellent alternative.

Note

Sesame oil is more easily removed from clothing than most other oils.

Figure 3.8   *Sesame plant (Sesamum indicum)*

Sunflower oil

The sunflower originated in South America although it is now grown in many countries. The flower head produces seeds. Sunflower oil is obtained from these seeds. The oil contains vitamins A, D and E, and minerals including calcium and iron.

Uses of sunflower oil

♦ Beneficial for skin complaints and bruises.

♦ Thought to be helpful for leg ulcers.

♦ Often used in preparations for acne and skin disorders in which there is dryness and inflammation, as it is softening and moisturising to the skin.

Wheatgerm oil

Note

Ensure the client is not allergic to wheat flour prior to using.

Wheatgerm oil is a cereal grass that is native to West Asia but also grown in other subtropical climates. The wheat grain at the top of the stem consists of the husk (bran), which surrounds the germ. The oil is extracted from the germ. It is not possible to achieve pure cold pressed oil so a process similar to maceration (see Calendula oil above) and also solvent extraction extracts it. The unrefined wheatgerm oil has a strong odour, which many people find unpleasant.

The oils contain high levels of vitamin E, which is a natural antioxidant (prevents oxidation), so can be added to other carrier oils to act as a preservative. Although fairly expensive, wheatgerm oil is the richest food source we have of vitamin E. The oil also contains vitamins A, B and also many minerals.

Although oxygen is essential to life it is also responsible for the deterioration (oxidation) of cells, such as skin cells. Antioxidants can help slow down this deterioration as they help prevent oxidation of the cells occurring.

Uses of wheatgerm oil

- Moisturises dry skins.

- Relieves symptoms of dermatitis.

- Beneficial for tired muscles, so is useful to use after exercise.

- It is useful on ageing skin due to its natural antioxidants, so helps prevent oxidation of the cells, which causes the skin to wrinkle and age.

- It is softening to the skin and acts as a cell regenerator, thus improving the condition of the skin.

Wheatgerm oil is often added to the carrier oil in the proportion of 10 per cent to 90 per cent of the main carrier oil (eg sweet almond). Adding 5 per cent or less wheatgerm oil to the aromatherapy blend will help preserve the oils as it prevents oxidisation of the blend.

Note

All vegetable carrier oils will go off and become rancid, and become unfit to use. They should be kept cool and not mixed with the essential oils until required for treatment.

Complete the table by giving two uses for each carrier oil.

Table 3.4 *Uses of carrier oils*

Carrier oil	Uses
Sweet almond	
Apricot	
Avocado	
Calendula	
Coconut	
Evening primrose	
Grapeseed	
Jojoba	
Macadamia	
Olive	
Peach	
Sesame	
Sunflower	
Wheatgerm	

Write your answers to the questions below, then check against the sample answers on the web site (www.saloneducation.co.uk).

1. List six common methods of using the essential oils.

   _____

   _____

   _____

   _____

   _____

   _____

2. Name three types of mask and give a brief description.

   _____

   _____

   _____

   _____

   _____

   _____

3. What proportion of essential and carrier oil would you mix to ensure a safe blend?

   _____

   _____

   _____

4. Briefly discuss essential oils and their use on the hair.

   _____

   _____

   _____

   _____

   _____

5. What is meant by the term synergy?

   _____

   _____

6. What is a carrier oil and what considerations would you take into account when purchasing a carrier oil?

   _____

   _____

   _____

   _____

   _____

7. List five carrier oils commonly used in aromatherapy.

   _____

   _____

   _____

   _____

   _____

Extraction methods

Essential oils are obtained from various parts of a plant, such as the flowers, leaves, wood and seeds. They are extracted from the plant by various methods. The main method is steam distillation; others include expression, enfleurage, solvent extraction, percolation and carbon dioxide extraction.

Steam distillation

- The plant parts are either heated in water or steam can be passed through the plant material.

- The heat and steam cause oil cells in the plant to be broken down. The resultant steam and oil vapours rise to the top of the vessel and are taken by pipe to another container.

- They are cooled, causing them to become a liquid, which is collected in vats.

- The water, mostly being heavier than the oil, drops to the bottom of the container and this may later be used as floral water, also called a hydrolat.

- At the top of the vat is the essential oil, which is now drawn off and collected.

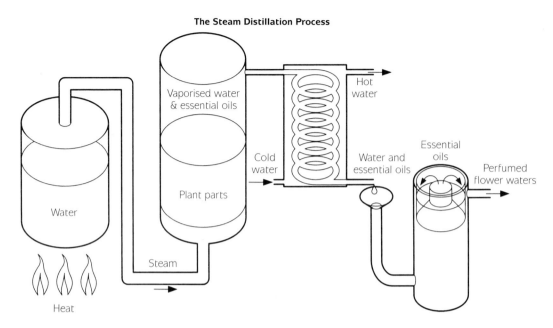

Figure 4.1 *Steam distillation of oils*

Hydrolats

Hydrolats are the by-product of the distillation process, often made with spring water. They contain a small amount of essential oil; about 2 g in a litre, which is dispersed. Hydrolats have similar properties to the corresponding essential oil and can be used neat on the skin. They are ideal to use as skin toners. The following are types of hydrolats:

Table 4.1: Types of hydrolat

Hydrolat	Skin type suitable to use on
Rose water	Normal, combination and sensitive skin
Lavender water	Greasy and combination skins
Chamomile water	Dry and inflamed skins
Neroli water	Normal and dry skins
Tea tree water	Acne and infected skin conditions

Hydrolats can be mixed with other essential oils but will not mix with carrier oils or vegetable based creams. They are mostly clear but may have slight colour, ranging from light pink to light purple. They should be stored in a cool, dark place, preferably a fridge. Most hydrolats can be stored for two to three years.

Expression

Traditionally this method was used to obtain oils from citrus fruits. The fruit peel was squeezed by hand, which released the oil and was then collected in sponges. Nowadays, this method may be carried out by machinery or, rarely, by hand, although it is said that the best quality citrus oils are extracted by hand. Either way, pressure is applied to the peel of the citrus fruits, such as lemon, bergamot and orange, to obtain the oil.

Enfleurage

Less than 10 per cent of essential oils are now produced by this method, which is time-consuming and expensive. Most oils are now produced by solvent extraction. It is therefore only used for more expensive oils from delicate blooms, such as rose and jasmine.

- Purified and odourless fat is spread in a thin layer over sheets of glass in wooden frames.

- The fat is covered with the petals of freshly gathered flowers and the frames are then stacked. The petals are removed when they have faded and are replaced with fresh petals.

- The process continues for several days, or even weeks in the case of jasmine, until the fat is thoroughly saturated with the essence of the petals. The term pomade is used to describe the mixture of fat and essential oil.

- This pomade of fat is washed in alcohol, which is then evaporated or shaken vigorously to separate the essential oil from the fat. What remains is known as an enfleurage.

Oils produced by this method are known as 'absolutes' and are highly concentrated essential oils. Their scent and properties are very strong and so smaller amounts are required to give the same effect as steam distilled oils. The absolute will be thicker in consistency than essential oils. Some absolutes, such as rose, solidify at room temperature and will turn to liquid when the bottle is gently warmed. The solvent extraction method also produces absolutes.

Solvent extraction

Solvent extraction method is a gentle extraction method and is used mainly where steam distillation would spoil the delicate fragrance of the plant part (an example is jasmine) or if the essential oil is difficult to obtain by distillation (for example, a resinoid such as benzoin).

Note

Resins are products obtained from the sap of certain trees and plants.

- A liquid solvent, such as liquid butane or liquid carbon dioxide, is used to dissolve the essential oils from the flowers or other parts of the plant.

- When the solvent is removed, the material that is left is semi-solid and is called a concrete. The concrete is a combination of the plant's natural waxes and essential oil or a resinous substance containing resin, depending on the plant part extracted.

- The concrete contains the aromatic material from the plant and is washed with pure alcohol. The alcohol is then evaporated or shaken to remove the plant waxes and a high quality absolute is left behind.

Note

Some of the finest flower absolutes are produced by means of solvent extraction.

Some aromatherapists do not like to use absolutes because the extraction method may cause traces of the solvents to remain in the absolute and these substances may cause skin irritation. An exception is where natural ethanol has been used.

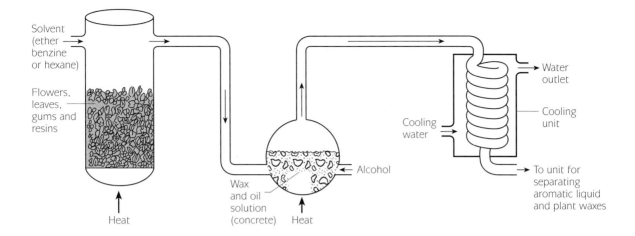

Solvent
(ether
benzine
or hexane)

Flowers,
leaves,
gums and
resins

Heat

Wax
and oil
solution
(concrete)

Heat

Alcohol

Cooling
water

Water
outlet

Cooling
unit

To unit for
separating
aromatic liquid
and plant waxes

Figure 4.2   *Solvent extraction of essential oils*

Hydrodiffusion/percolation

Hydrodiffusion is a relatively new way of extracting
essential oils from plants. It is similar to steam distillation
but the steam passes down through the plant rather than
up. The steam and vapours pass through a pipe into
cooling tanks. As with steam distillation the essential oils
are drawn off at the end of the process.

This method is useful for extracting essential oils from
woody and tough plant parts, such as seeds. This method
is a great deal quicker than the original steam distillation
method. It also produces better quality oil as the shorter
time in contact with the steams means less damage to the
plant parts.

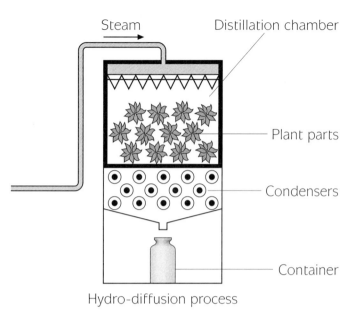

Steam   Distillation chamber

Plant parts

Condensers

Container

Hydro-diffusion process

Figure 4.3 *The Hydrodiffusion process*

Carbon dioxide extraction

This method of extraction has been used since the 1980s. The plant part is brought into contact with compressed carbon dioxide at a low temperature. The low temperature ensures the essential oil is not affected by heat, as may occur in the distillation process. The process is quick and there will be no contamination of the oils but it is quite complex and expensive because of the equipment needed. The oils extracted by this process are said to be of a high quality.

Write a brief description of each extraction method below:

Extraction method	Brief description
Steam distillation	_____
	_____
Expression	_____
	_____
Enfleurage	_____
	_____
Solvent extraction	_____
	_____
Percolation/hydrodiffusion	_____
	_____
Carbon dioxide	_____
	_____

Botanical classification of plants

Plants are divided into families. The system of plant classification helps to identify a particular plant and its properties. The table below shows a selection of botanical families and the plants to which they belong.

Table 4.2   The botanical classification of plants

Botanical family	Examples	Notes
Labitae (Lamiaceae)	Basil, clary sage, lavender, marjoram, melissa, origanum, patchouli, peppermint, rosemary, sage and thyme	This is the biggest plant family from which essential oils are taken. These plants are strongly aromatic.
Cupressaceae	Cypress, juniper and pine	
Styraceae	The resinoid called benzoin	

Botanical family	Examples	Notes
Rosaceae	Rose otto (rose damask)	
Valerianaceae	Valerian	
Rutaceae	Citrus oils such as bergamot, lemon and grapefruit	In this family the oils are extracted from the peel, flower and leaf.
Umbelliferae (Apiaceae)	Fennel, which is known for its digestive properties	In this family the oils are usually extracted from seeds.
Poaceae or Gramineae	Lemongrass, palmarosa and vetiver	
Piperaceae	Black pepper	
Burseraceae	Frankincense (olibanum) and myrrh	
Oleaceae	Jasmine	
Compositae (Asteraceae)	Calendula and the chamomiles	The essential oils from these plants are taken from the flowerheads.
Myrtaceae	Cajuput, eucalyptus, clove and tea tree	The essential oils from this family are taken from the cells in the leaf.
Geranacea	Geranium	
Lauraceae	Cinnamon, rosewood and camphor	
Anonaceae	This family consists of only one species – ylang-ylang	

Essential oil chemicals

An essential oil contains over one hundred different chemical constituents. Almost all of the molecules found in essential oils are composed of carbon, hydrogen and oxygen. Essential oils are organic compounds, which means they all contain carbon. The study of carbon-based chemicals is known as organic chemistry.

Molecules are made up of atoms joined together. To take the example of CO_2 (carbon dioxide). There is one carbon atom (C) and two oxygen atoms (O_2). The joining of the carbon atom and the oxygen atoms makes one molecule.

The joining of different molecules will create different chemicals as found in essential oils. Chemicals found in essential oils include terpenes, alcohols, aldehydes, esters, ketones, oxides and phenols. These various chemicals can have beneficial properties on the body.

Terpenes are known as hydrocarbons, as they contain molecules of hydrogen and carbon. Alcohols, aldehydes, esters, ketones, oxides and phenols are known as oxygenated compounds, as they contain hydrogen, carbon and oxygen.

Understanding the actions of these chemicals will help you to know what properties an essential oil will have.

Table 4.3   Essential oil chemicals and their properties

Essential oil chemical	Properties described on pages 70–2	Examples	Notes
Terpenes	Are found in almost all essential oils but their effects are quite weak. Two types of terpenes are monoterpenes and sesquiterpenes		
Monoterpenes	Antiseptic in the air, antiviral, slightly analgesic, expectorant, stimulate the adrenal glands, rubefacient, useful for skin hygiene, generally stimulating	Citrus oils contain high amounts of monoterpenes. Other examples include limonene found in fennel, pine, frankincense and neroli. Pinene found in pine, lemon and frankincense and ocimene found in basil and sweet marjoram.	Can be aggressive to the skin and mucous membranes such as the mouth and nose. Evaporate easily and oxidise quickly. Weak odour. Have names ending in 'ene'.

Table 4.3 (cont.)   Essential oil chemicals and their properties

Essential oil chemical	Properties described on pages 70–2	Examples	Notes
Sesquiterpenes	Antiseptic, hypotensive, bactericidal, calming	Chamazulene is an excellent anti-inflammatory and is found in chamomiles. Caryophyllene is found in lavender, marjoram and clary sage.	As with all terpenes, the properties are generally weak. Strong odour, so determine the fragrance of an oil. Have names ending in 'ene'.
Alcohols	Anti-inflammatory, strong bactericides, antiseptic, antiviral, antirheumatic and calming	Linalol is found in rosewood and lavender. Geraniol is found in geranium and santalol is found in sandalwood.	Alcohols have names ending in 'ol'.
Aldehydes	Antiseptic, anti-inflammatory, antirheumatic, tonic, sedative and calming to the nervous system. Some lower blood pressure and others help reduce a fever	Found mainly in lemon-scented essences like lemongrass, melissa and citronella. Citronellal is found in citronella and citral is found in lemongrass.	Have a fruity odour. Can be skin irritants and sensitisers. Have names ending in 'al' or the word 'aldehyde' included in their name.
Esters	Anti-inflammatory, antifungal, antispasmodic, sedative and calming. Tonic to the nervous system. Useful for skin problems	Geranyl acetate is found in sweet marjoram. Linalyl acetate is found in bergamot, clary sage and lavender. Benzyl benzoate is found in benzoin.	Found in most essential oils and usually have a fruity aroma. Highest levels of esters are produced when flowers are in full bloom and fruits or plants have reached maturity. Have names ending in 'yl' or 'ate'.
Ketones, (also known as camphor)	Excellent mucolytic effects; sedative, healing, decongestant, immuno-stimulant, antifungal.	Non toxic ketones include camphor, found in rosemary, and fenchone, found in fennel.	High levels are toxic to the central nervous system, abortifacient and may bring on an epileptic fit. Use well diluted and with care. Names ending in 'one'.

Table 4.3 (cont.)   Essential oil chemicals and their properties

Essential oil chemical	Properties described on pages 70–2	Examples	Notes
Oxides	Expectorant, decongestant, stimulating and warming	Cineole is found in eucalyptus, rosemary, tea tree and cajeput.	Found in many essential oils. Names end in 'ole'.
Phenols	Antibacterial, antifungal and antiviral, stimulating to nervous and immune systems	Thymol and cavacrol are found in thyme and eugenol is found in clove and black pepper.	Essential oils containing relatively large amounts of phenols may irritate the skin. If used in large amounts over a long period of time may damage the liver. Phenol names end in 'ol', so do not confuse them with the alcohol names.

Task 4.2

Using the information above, state three properties of each chemical below:

Chemical	Three properties of chemical
Monoterpenes	_____
Sesquiterpenes	_____
Alcohols	_____
Aldehydes	_____
Esters	_____
Ketones	_____
Oxides	_____
Phenols	_____

Chemotypes

Essential oils can be extracted from two identical plants, such as from two rosemary plants that are of the same variety, but each can vary in chemical make-up. These plants have had nothing added or taken away from the natural essential oil. The variation can be due to factors such as where it is grown, climate, season and soil type.

Sometimes this variation can cause changes in the properties of the essential oils. These plants are known as chemotypes. A thyme plant is a typical example of a chemotype and some wholesalers list over three chemotypes of thyme oil.

Quality of essential oils

Suppliers should carry out frequent tests to check the quality of the essential oils. The most common method is gas liquid chromatography (GLC). Chromatography is the method of separating substances in a mixture; therefore it will show the chemical make-up of the essential oils. It is used to separate an essential oil into its individual constituents and the results can be printed as shown in the diagrams below.

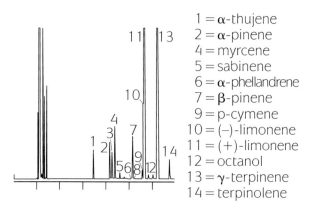

1 = α-thujene
2 = α-pinene
4 = myrcene
5 = sabinene
6 = α-phellandrene
7 = β-pinene
9 = p-cymene
10 = (−)-limonene
11 = (+)-limonene
12 = octanol
13 = γ-terpinene
14 = terpinolene

Figure 4.4 *Gas chromatogram of a mandarin essential oil*

Testing

To test the purity of essential oils a small quantity of the oil is injected on to a fine, coiled, tubular column and is filled with an absorbent material. The coil has gas flowing through it and is fitted within a temperature-controlled oven. The heat causes the lighter components to be carried along the column more rapidly. The time taken for each component to pass along the column is called the retention time. The chromatogram for each batch of essential oils is compared with an original copy and the addition or absence of peaks may indicate that the oil has been adulterated. Each essential oil is given a certificate stating its authenticity and batch number to confirm its purity after testing.

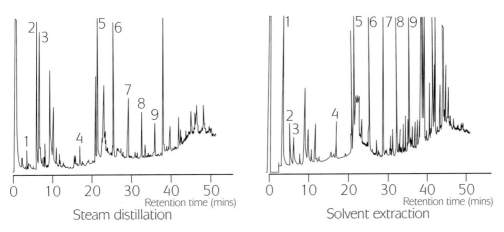

Chromatograms of the various rose extracts.
1. Phenyl ethyl alcohol, 2. Citronellol, 3. Geraniol, C17-C27 Hydrocarbons. Notice that the main body of the rose extact 'Phenyl ethyl alcohol' is lost in the steam distillation process.

Figure 4.5 *Chromatogram of rose essential oil, using two extraction methods*

Note

Essential oils should totally evaporate when placed on to paper. If an oily stain remains then the essential oil has been mixed with a vegetable oil.

Adulteration

It is important that essential oils are bought from reputable suppliers, otherwise there is a risk that the essential oil has been adulterated in some way. There are different ways in which essential oils can be adulterated; synthetic chemicals that look and smell similar to the essential oil it is imitating can be included or a cheaper oil may be added to a more expensive oil. The following essential oils can be adulterated by adding a cheaper essential oil.

Table 4.4   Essential oils that can be adulterated

Cheaper oil	More expensive oil
Petitgrain can be added to	neroli
Palmarosa can be added to	rose otto, rose maroc
Cedarwood can be added to	sandalwood
Lemongrass can be added to	melissa

Adulterating these oils will have an effect on the essential oil's beneficial properties. It is almost impossible to reproduce the oils synthetically as they are highly complex in structure.

Properties of essential oils

All essential oils have therapeutic properties, which make them useful for treating certain ailments and conditions. The properties are shown in the table below.

Table 4.5   Properties of essential oils

Property	Description
Analgesic	Helps to relieve pain
Adrenal cortex stimulant	Stimulates hormones from the adrenal cortex
Anti-allergic	Helps to prevent allergic reactions
Antibacterial/bactericidal	Helps to destroy bacteria
Antidepressant	Helps to alleviate depression

Table 4.5 (cont.)   Properties of essential oils

Property	Description
Antifungal/fungicide	Helps to destroy fungi
Anti-inflammatory	Helps to reduce inflammation
Antimicrobial	Destroys micro-organisms
Anti-oxidant	Helps to prevent oxidation (oxidation means to combine with oxygen), which will cause ageing of body cells
Antiseborrhoeic	Helps to reduce the amount of sebum produced
Antiseptic	Prevents or helps fight infection
Antispasmodic	Helps to relieve spasms
Antitoxic	Helps to work against the effects of poison
Antiviral	Helps to destroy viruses
Aperitif	Helps to stimulate appetite
Aphrodisiac	Helps to promote sexual desire
Astringent	Helps to contract and tighten tissues, especially of the skin
Balsamic	Helps to soothe and heal an area
Carminative	Settles the digestive system and relieves flatulence
Cell regenerator/ cytophylactic	Helps to promote division of cells such as in the skin
Cephalic	Helps to clear the mind
Circulatory stimulant	Stimulates the blood circulation
Deodorant	Helps to mask or remove unpleasant odours
Detoxifying	Helps to remove toxins from the body
Digestive	Aids digestion of food
Diuretic	Increases the amount of urine produced
Emmenagogue	Promotes menstruation
Expectorant	Helps to remove mucus from respiratory tract
Febrifuge	Helps to reduce temperature such as during a fever
Haemostatic	Helps to stop bleeding

Table 4.5 (cont.)   Properties of essential oils

Property	Description
Hormone balancer	Helps to maintain the balance of hormones
Hypertensive	Increases blood pressure so is useful for poor circulation
Hypotensive	Lowers blood pressure by dilating the arteries
Immuno-stimulant	Stimulates the immune system
Insecticide	Helps to kill insects
Insect repellent	Helps to repel insects
Nervine relaxant	Helps to relax the nervous system
Neuro-tonic/nervine tonic	Helps to strengthen the nervous system
Oestrogen stimulant	Helps to stimulate the production of oestrogen
Parasiticide	Helps to kill parasites
Rehydrating	If the skin is dry and lacks moisture it helps to rehydrate the skin
Relaxant	Helps to induce relaxation of the body and mind
Rubefacient	Warms an area and causes erythema, therefore there are increased oxygen and nutrients
Sedative	Helps to calm the nervous system so is useful for stress sufferers
Stimulant	Stimulates a particular system or the whole body
Tonic	Strengthens a certain part of the body or the whole of it, e.g. nerve tonic
Uplifting	Helps to uplift the emotions
Vulnerary	Helps wounds to heal more quickly

Effects of essential oils on body systems

Now that you understand the properties you will be able to understand the effects that essential oils have on the body's systems.

Effects on the skin

Essential oils can greatly improve the health of the skin.

- They improve elasticity of the skin so that the skin's stretchiness improves. The elasticity of the skin reduces with age.

- They help reduce the incidence of stretch marks.

- They help to heal scar tissue.

- They encourage cell division in the basal layer, which improves the health of the skin. Such oils are known as cytophylatic oils, which can include lavender and neroli.

- They desquamate the skin (rub off the dead skin cells), especially when applied with massage.

- They help to clear spots and improve acne skin.

- Anti-inflammatory properties of oils help to reduce inflammation, i.e. psoriasis or bruising.

- Antiseborrhoeic properties help control the amount of sebum released, so can improve oily skin types. Geranium is a balancing oil so is especially useful for oily or dry skins.

- They help to improve dry skin conditions, as certain essential oils such as geranium can help regulate the secretion of sebum.

- Some essential oils have rehydrating properties so can help restore moisture to the skin.

- Oils with antiseptic properties help to treat insect bites, cuts and wounds.

> **Note**
>
> Chapter 5 lists the essential oils that can be useful for treating conditions relating to each bodily system.

Effects on the circulatory system

Essential oils travel in the blood and can have positive effects on the circulatory systems.

- Some of the oils can have a calming and relaxing effect, so can help if high blood pressure is stress-

Note

To understand the effects of stress on the bodily systems see Chapter 1.

related. Oils with hypotensive properties are useful to help treat high blood pressure.

♦ Certain essential oils will help to stimulate the blood circulation, therefore aid poor circulation.

♦ Rubefacient properties help to widen the blood capillaries and so more blood can pass through them. The blood will bring the oxygen and nutrients necessary to repair damaged muscle tissues.

Effects on the immune system

Essential oils can be beneficial to the immune system by helping to stimulate the body's immune system. Such oils are known as immuno-stimulant oils, and so strengthen the body's defences against diseases caused by bacteria and viruses. Useful oils include bergamot, clove, eucalyptus, lavender, lemon, pine, rosemary, tea tree and thyme.

Effects on the lymphatic system

There are essential oils that are useful for conditions associated with the lymphatic system. This system plays an important role in the immune response to harmful substances in the body.

♦ Almost all essential oils increase the production of white blood cells to stimulate immunity, but the best oils for this are lavender, chamomile, rosemary, bergamot and tea tree.

♦ Certain oils act as diuretics, helping to eliminate the build-up of fluid. Fluid retention is a common problem and causes swelling, often seen around the ankles. This is also known as oedema and can be differentiated from other types of swelling by the fact that slight pressure will leave a dent, which takes a few seconds to return to normal and is usually not uncomfortable if touched.

♦ Cellulite is often seen on the thighs and buttocks, and is caused by deposits of fat, which give the skin a dimpled, pitted appearance. There is retention of toxic waste and fluids in the affected area, and this condition is also related to sluggish lymph circulation. Using oils that are diuretics and applying massage strokes towards the groups of lymph nodes in the abdominal and groin areas will aid lymphatic drainage, and help treat fluid retention and cellulite conditions.

Effects on the skeletal/muscular system

Essential oils can be beneficial for the skeletal and muscular system.

♦ In the case of arthritis, uric acid crystals deposit in the joint spaces causing inflammation, stiffness and pain. Detoxifying oils can help to eliminate these toxins and relieve these symptoms. Many oils have anti-inflammatory properties, so will help to reduce inflammation around joints.

♦ Essential oils can help to heal muscle fibres that are slightly torn, maybe due to vigorous exercise or minor injury. Many oils also have analgesic (pain-relieving) properties that will help to reduce muscular, tendon and ligament pain.

♦ Certain essential oils have antispasmodic properties, so will help to relieve muscular spasm, and also have a relaxing effect on the smooth muscle of the internal organs. These oils can be used to relieve problems such as indigestion, colic, menstrual cramps and diarrhoea, which involve spasm of smooth muscle.

Note

Use a hot compress to relieve smooth muscle spasm.

♦ Some oils have a rubefacient effect, which causes an increase in blood supply and therefore an increase in oxygen and nutrients, which will help to heal injured muscle. This will mean an increase in the removal of waste products such as lactic acid, which may be the cause of muscular tension.

Effects on the nervous system

♦ Oils with an analgesic effect help to relieve pain by damping down the activity of the nerve endings that transmit pain.

Note

Many sedative oils are also analgesic and antispasmodic, so are very useful in treating the nervous system. These oils include chamomile, lavender and marjoram.

- Oils that have cephalic properties help to clear the mind, aid concentration and memory, and are also useful for mental fatigue.

- Certain oils can reduce nervous tension and help with stress-related conditions.

- Oils with neurotonic (also called nervine) properties help to strengthen the whole nervous system. Anxiety, insomnia, shock and stress-related problems all benefit from using these oils.

- Anxiety and stress can lead to cardiovascular problems. The use of oils that are relaxants will help to reduce stress and anxiety. These include bergamot, lavender, chamomile and frankincense.

Effects on the endocrine system

Certain essential oils contain plant hormones called phytohormones, which act in a similar way to human hormones when they enter the bloodstream. Fennel contains the female hormone oestrogen and is helpful for pre-menstrual syndrome and the menopause. Oestrogen is needed by men and women to maintain muscle tone, elasticity of the skin and connective tissue, a healthy blood circulation and strong bones.

Note

Lavender can help to calm the heart and mind and so prevent palpitations from occurring if they are induced through anxiety.

Effects on the respiratory system

Respiratory disorders such as asthma, bronchitis and chest infections can all be helped by the use of essential oils.

- Anti-inflammatory properties help treat the inflammation associated with bronchitis and sinusitis.

- Expectorants are useful to help remove mucus build-up and therefore assist the respiratory system.

- Antibacterial oils are useful to help fight or prevent infections of the respiratory system.

- Antiviral oils are useful to help fight or prevent viral infections of the respiratory system.

- Antispasmodic oils such as clary sage, frankincense and peppermint can help calm spasm in the bronchial tubes.

Note

Do not recommend an inhalation treatment to someone suffering with asthma, as it could trigger an asthma attack.

Effects on the digestive system

Baths and massage to the abdominal area can help with conditions such as excessive wind and constipation. The massage has to be carried out in a clockwise direction (following the direction of the colon).

- Oils with antispasmodic properties help to relieve pain associated with intestinal spasm, often a symptom of irritable bowel syndrome.

- Carminatives help to relax the stomach muscles, reduce the production of gas and increase peristalsis of the intestine.

- Hepatics help to strengthen the liver and stimulate its secretions.

- Digestive properties in oils aid the digestion of food through the intestines so can help prevent colic, flatulence and indigestion.

Effects on the reproductive system

Essential oils are very useful for females for pre-menstrual syndrome, pregnancy and menopause.

- Emmenagogues help to promote menstruation and so assist the elimination of menstrual blood. Amenorrhoea (lack of periods) can be caused by shock, menopause, hormone imbalance and coming on and off the contraceptive pill.

- Oestrogen stimulant properties of some oils will help stimulate the production of oestrogen, so they are useful at the menopause and to help stimulate or regulate menstruation.

Effects on the urinary system

- Oils with antiseptic properties will help to treat cystitis.

- Diuretics help to promote urination, therefore assisting the excretory functions of the kidneys.

Note

Peppermint oil is used in Colpermin, a medicine commonly used to treat the symptoms of irritable bowel syndrome.

Note

Many common digestive problems can be improved or avoided by changes of lifestyle and habits.

State two effects that the essential oils have on each of the body's systems given below.

Body systems	Two effects
Skin	
Circulatory	
Lymphatic/immune	
Skeletal	
Muscular	
Nervous	
Respiratory	
Digestive	
Reproductive	
Urinary	

Write your answers to the questions below, then check against the sample answers on the website (www.saloneducation.co.uk).

1. What are hydrolats?

_____

_____

_____

_____

2. What is an absolute?

_____

_____

_____

_____

3. Explain what is meant by the botanical classification of plants?

_____

_____

_____

_____

4. What is meant by a chemotype?

_____

_____

_____

_____

_____

5. What do the letters GLC stand for and what is the purpose of this process?

_____

_____

_____

_____

_____

6. Name two ways in which essential oils can be adulterated.

_____

_____

_____

_____

_____

The essential oils

The following pages contain information about each of the main essential oils that you are likely to use. This includes the plant from which the oil is taken, its chemical make-up, particular uses or properties and situations in which the oil should not be used.

The oils covered include:

Basil
Benzoin
Bergamot
Black pepper
Cajeput
Carrot seed
Cedarwood
Chamomile (German)
Chamomile (Maroc)
Chamomile (Roman)
Clary sage
Clove
Cypress
Eucalyptus
Fennel
Frankincense
Geranium
Ginger
Grapefruit
Jasmine
Juniper

Lavender
Lemon
Lemongrass
Mandarin
Marjoram
Melissa
Myrrh
Neroli
Orange
Patchouli
Peppermint
Petitgrain
Pine
Rose (cabbage)
Rose (damask)
Rosemary
Sandalwood
Tea tree
Thyme
Valerian
Veliver
Ylang-ylang

OCIMUM BASILICUM – BASIL (FRENCH)

- **Plant description:** Herb with green leaves and small white/pink flowers
- **Botanical family:** Lamiaceae
- **Note:** Top
- **Extraction:** Steam distillation of the leaves and flowering tops
- **Production:** Originated in Asia and Africa, now grown widely across Europe, including France and Italy
- **Blends well with:** Bergamot, black pepper, clary sage, clove, eucalyptus, fennel, geranium, ginger, juniper, lavender, lemon, marjoram, orange and rosemary

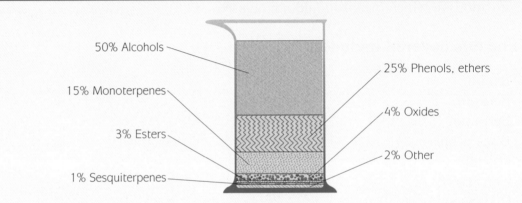

50% Alcohols
25% Phenols, ethers
15% Monoterpenes
4% Oxides
3% Esters
2% Other
1% Sesquiterpenes

Notes

- There are four main types of basil essential oils, including exotic, French, methyl cinnamate and eugenol basil. French basil is said to be the best quality basil.

- French basil, also known as European basil, is used instead of exotic basil because it contains lower amounts of methyl chavicol (phenols), so is therefore less toxic than exotic basil.

- Basil could help to reduce some allergies as it has an effect on the adrenal cortex, which controls allergies that are related to stress.

- Basil encourages concentration and sharpens the senses, so is useful when taking exams.

Caution

- Avoid in pregnancy.
- Do not use on epileptics.
- May irritate sensitive skins.

Basil (French)

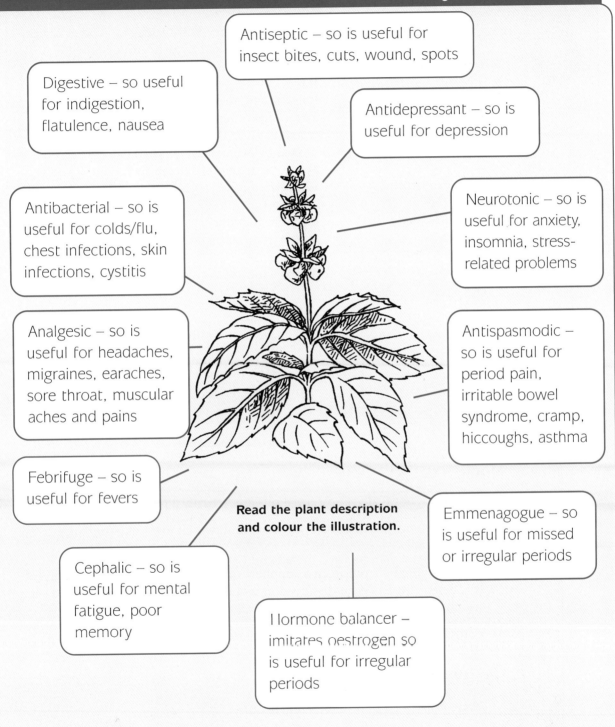

Antiseptic – so is useful for insect bites, cuts, wound, spots

Digestive – so useful for indigestion, flatulence, nausea

Antidepressant – so is useful for depression

Antibacterial – so is useful for colds/flu, chest infections, skin infections, cystitis

Neurotonic – so is useful for anxiety, insomnia, stress-related problems

Analgesic – so is useful for headaches, migraines, earaches, sore throat, muscular aches and pains

Antispasmodic – so is useful for period pain, irritable bowel syndrome, cramp, hiccoughs, asthma

Febrifuge – so is useful for fevers

Read the plant description and colour the illustration.

Emmenagogue – so is useful for missed or irregular periods

Cephalic – so is useful for mental fatigue, poor memory

Hormone balancer – imitates oestrogen so is useful for irregular periods

STYRAX BENZOIN – BENZOIN

- **Plant description:** Large tropical tree with pale green leaves bearing small, hard-shelled flattish fruit
- **Botanical family:** Styracaceae
- **Note:** Base
- **Extraction:** Incisions are made into the bark of the tree and sap exudes from the cuts. This greyish brown, resinous lump is pressed into a solid mass and melted by heating over water before it can be used. Solvent extraction of the resin produces benzoin.
- **Production:** Originated in Asia. Cultivated in Indonesia and Thailand.
- **Blends well with:** Cypress, frankincense, juniper, lavender, lemon, myrrh, rose and sandalwood

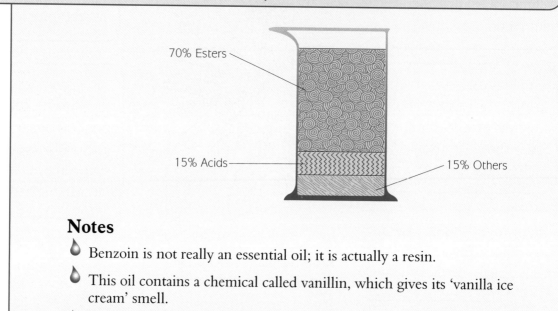

70% Esters

15% Acids

15% Others

Notes

- Benzoin is not really an essential oil; it is actually a resin.

- This oil contains a chemical called vanillin, which gives its 'vanilla ice cream' smell.

- When buying benzoin from a supplier it is usually dissolved in ethyl glycol. It is better if it has been dissolved in wood alcohol or bought in a solid state and melted when needed.

- Benzoin is often used as a fixative in perfume to help prolong the aroma.

Caution

- May cause sensitisation in some people.

- Can have a drowsy effect.

Benzoin

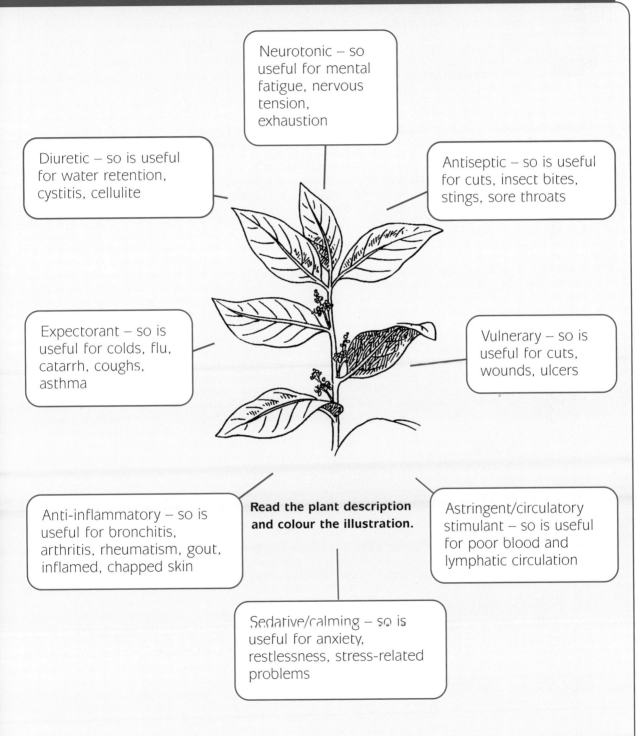

Neurotonic – so useful for mental fatigue, nervous tension, exhaustion

Diuretic – so is useful for water retention, cystitis, cellulite

Antiseptic – so is useful for cuts, insect bites, stings, sore throats

Expectorant – so is useful for colds, flu, catarrh, coughs, asthma

Vulnerary – so is useful for cuts, wounds, ulcers

Anti-inflammatory – so is useful for bronchitis, arthritis, rheumatism, gout, inflamed, chapped skin

Read the plant description and colour the illustration.

Astringent/circulatory stimulant – so is useful for poor blood and lymphatic circulation

Sedative/calming – so is useful for anxiety, restlessness, stress-related problems

CITRUS BERGAMIA – BERGAMOT

- **Plant description:** Small tree with oval green leaves bearing small fruit, which ripens from green to yellow and is similar in appearance to a small orange
- **Botanical family:** Rutaceae
- **Note:** Top
- **Extraction:** Expression of the peel of a small, pear-shaped, green/yellow fruit
- **Production:** Originated from tropical Asia. Now grown in southern Italy
- **Blends well with:** Most essential oils including black pepper, clary sage, cypress, frankincense, geranium, orange, rosemary, vetiver, ylang-ylang

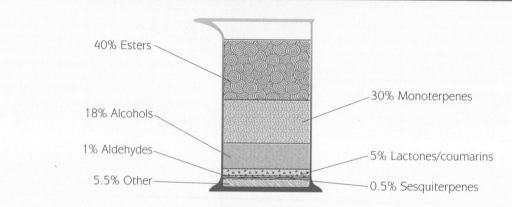

40% Esters
18% Alcohols
1% Aldehydes
5.5% Other
30% Monoterpenes
5% Lactones/coumarins
0.5% Sesquiterpenes

Notes

- The leaves of the bergamot tree are used to flavour Earl Grey tea.
- The bergamot tree is named after the town of Bergamo in Italy, where the oil was first sold.
- Bergamot is a common ingredient in perfumes, especially eau-de-Cologne.
- The bergamot fruit is not edible because the pulp is too sour.

Caution

May irritate the skin in high concentrations. Bergamot is phototoxic due to the chemical bergapten (a furocoumarin). A bergapten-free bergamot can be used instead.

Bergamot

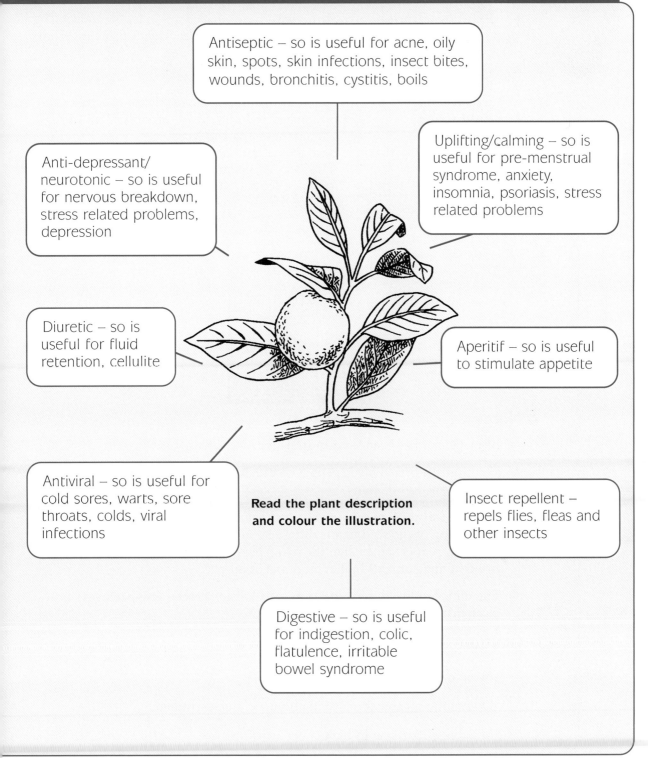

Antiseptic – so is useful for acne, oily skin, spots, skin infections, insect bites, wounds, bronchitis, cystitis, boils

Uplifting/calming – so is useful for pre-menstrual syndrome, anxiety, insomnia, psoriasis, stress related problems

Anti-depressant/ neurotonic – so is useful for nervous breakdown, stress related problems, depression

Diuretic – so is useful for fluid retention, cellulite

Aperitif – so is useful to stimulate appetite

Antiviral – so is useful for cold sores, warts, sore throats, colds, viral infections

Read the plant description and colour the illustration.

Insect repellent – repels flies, fleas and other insects

Digestive – so is useful for indigestion, colic, flatulence, irritable bowel syndrome

PIPER NIGRUM – BLACK PEPPER

- **Plant description:** Shrub with heart-shaped green leaves and small white flowers. It produces berries that turn from red to black as they mature.
- **Botanical family:** Piperaceae
- **Note:** Middle
- **Extraction:** Steam distillation of the nearly ripe berries
- **Production:** Originated in India. Major producers are India, China, Indonesia and Malaysia.
- **Blends well with:** Basil, bergamot, cajeput, cypress, eucalyptus, frankincense, geranium, ginger, grapefruit, lavender, lemon, marjoram, pine, rosemary, sandalwood, tea tree, ylang-ylang

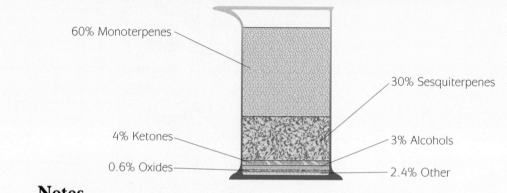

60% Monoterpenes
30% Sesquiterpenes
4% Ketones
3% Alcohols
0.6% Oxides
2.4% Other

Notes

- Black pepper has been used in India for over 4000 years.

- The Romans prized black pepper so much that taxes were often paid with this herb instead of coins.

- Black and white peppers are extracted from the same plant but it is the preparation of the seed that is different. The essential oil is extracted from the black pepper rather than the white pepper, as black pepper is more aromatic and contains higher amounts of oils.

- The oil is produced from the same small, black berries (peppercorns) as those that are used to season food.

Caution

- Avoid during pregnancy.

- Do not use on someone having homeopathic treatment.

- May cause irritation in high concentrations.

Black pepper

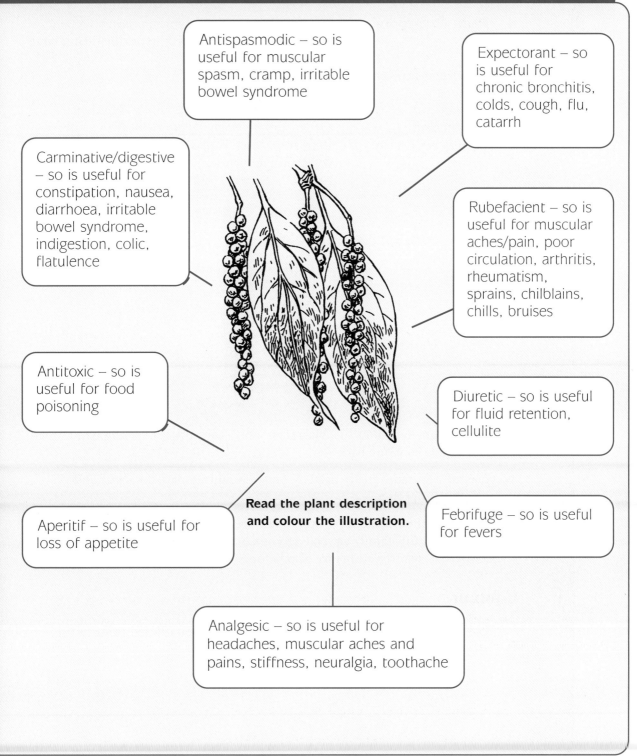

Antispasmodic – so is useful for muscular spasm, cramp, irritable bowel syndrome

Expectorant – so is useful for chronic bronchitis, colds, cough, flu, catarrh

Carminative/digestive – so is useful for constipation, nausea, diarrhoea, irritable bowel syndrome, indigestion, colic, flatulence

Rubefacient – so is useful for muscular aches/pain, poor circulation, arthritis, rheumatism, sprains, chilblains, chills, bruises

Antitoxic – so is useful for food poisoning

Diuretic – so is useful for fluid retention, cellulite

Read the plant description and colour the illustration.

Aperitif – so is useful for loss of appetite

Febrifuge – so is useful for fevers

Analgesic – so is useful for headaches, muscular aches and pains, stiffness, neuralgia, toothache

MELALEUCA CAJEPUTI – CAJEPUT

- **Plant description:** Tall evergreen tree with thick, pointed green leaves and white flowers. The flexible trunk has a whitish bark
- **Botanical family:** Myrtaceae
- **Note:** Top
- **Extraction:** Steam distillation of the leaves and buds
- **Production:** Originated in Malaysia and Australia
- **Blends well with:** Bergamot, black pepper, clove, eucalyptus, geranium, ginger, lemon, peppermint, pine, rosemary, tea tree, thyme

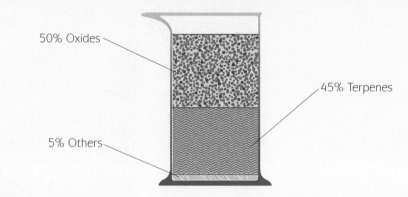

50% Oxides
45% Terpenes
5% Others

Notes

- Cajeput is named after the Malaysian word 'caju-puti', meaning white tree, referring to its white bark

- Cajeput was traditionally used by the aborigines for its antiseptic and analgesic properties.

- It is one of the Melaleuca group, a sub-species of the Myrtaceae family. All members of this family are able to combat and sometimes prevent infection. Eucalyptus, tea tree and clove also belong to this family.

Caution

- Non-toxic, but may irritate skin, so should be well diluted prior to use.

Cajeput

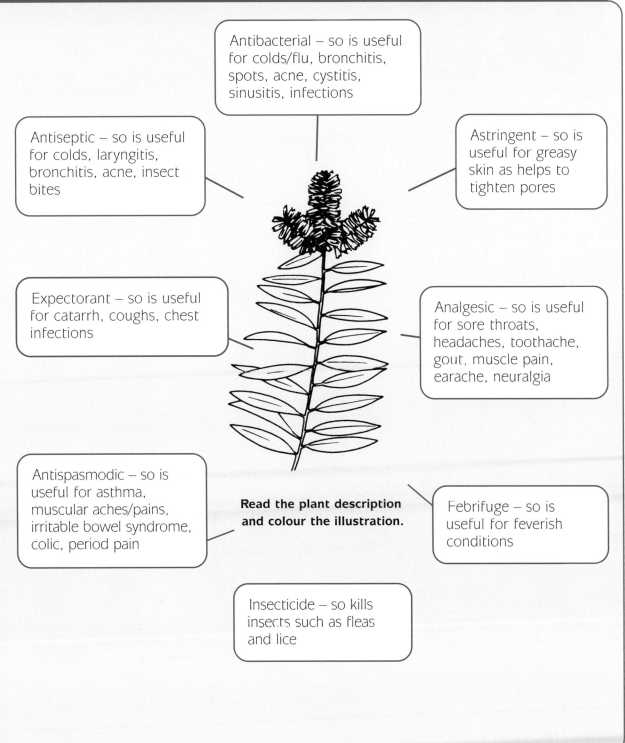

Antibacterial – so is useful for colds/flu, bronchitis, spots, acne, cystitis, sinusitis, infections

Antiseptic – so is useful for colds, laryngitis, bronchitis, acne, insect bites

Astringent – so is useful for greasy skin as helps to tighten pores

Expectorant – so is useful for catarrh, coughs, chest infections

Analgesic – so is useful for sore throats, headaches, toothache, gout, muscle pain, earache, neuralgia

Antispasmodic – so is useful for asthma, muscular aches/pains, irritable bowel syndrome, colic, period pain

Read the plant description and colour the illustration.

Febrifuge – so is useful for feverish conditions

Insecticide – so kills insects such as fleas and lice

DAUCUS CAROTA – CARROT SEED

- **Plant description:** Vegetable with green leaves and white flowers
- **Botanical family:** Umbelliferae
- **Note:** Middle
- **Extraction:** Solvent extraction of the orange root of the carrot
- **Production:** Originated in Europe, Asia, North Africa. France is now a main producer.
- **Blends well with:** Bergamot, cypress, fennel, geranium, grapefruit, juniper, lavender, lemon, mandarin, orange, rosemary, rose absolute, rose otto, sandalwood

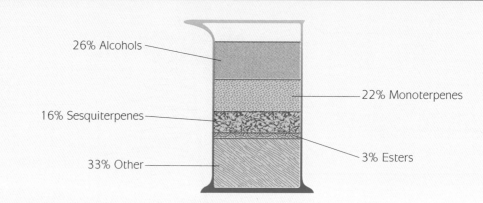

26% Alcohols
22% Monoterpenes
16% Sesquiterpenes
3% Esters
33% Other

Notes

The essential oil is obtained mainly from wild carrot, although it can be obtained from carrots we commonly eat.

Carrot seed is considered an excellent blood purifier, due to its detoxifying effect on the liver.

Carrot seed oil is rich in vitamins A, B$_1$, B$_2$ and C.

Caution

Avoid during pregnancy.

Carrot seed

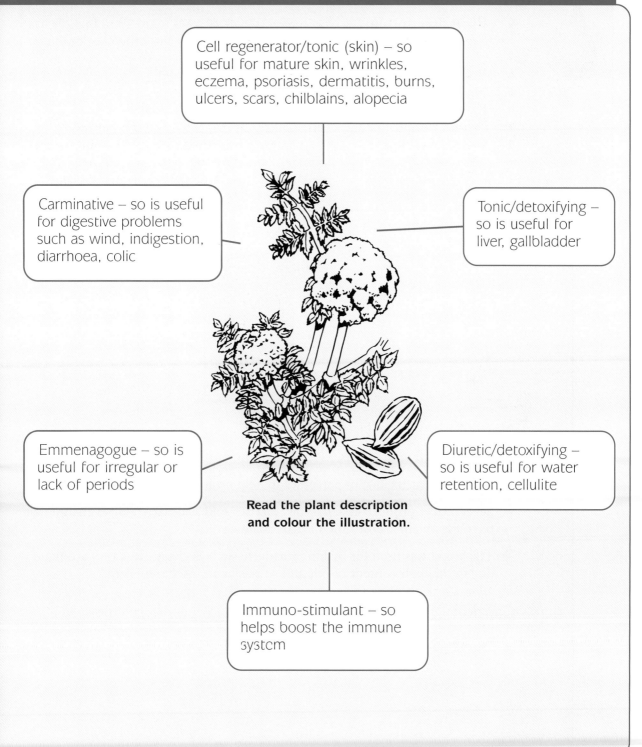

Cell regenerator/tonic (skin) – so useful for mature skin, wrinkles, eczema, psoriasis, dermatitis, burns, ulcers, scars, chilblains, alopecia

Carminative – so is useful for digestive problems such as wind, indigestion, diarrhoea, colic

Tonic/detoxifying – so is useful for liver, gallbladder

Emmenagogue – so is useful for irregular or lack of periods

Diuretic/detoxifying – so is useful for water retention, cellulite

Read the plant description and colour the illustration.

Immuno-stimulant – so helps boost the immune system

CEDRUS ATLANTICA – CEDARWOOD (ATLAS)

- **Plant description:** Evergreen tree that grows up to 40 m high. It has small, green, spiky leaves and brown-coloured cones.
- **Botanical family:** Pinaceae
- **Note:** Base
- **Extraction:** Steam distillation of the wood
- **Production:** Originates from Morocco and the Lebanon
- **Blends well with:** Bergamot, cypress, frankincense, jasmine, juniper, lavender, lemon, neroli, patchouli, orange, sandalwood, rose, rosemary, vetiver and ylang-ylang

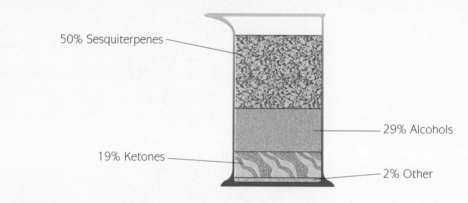

50% Sesquiterpenes

29% Alcohols

19% Ketones

2% Other

Notes

- Egyptians often used this oil for embalming in mummification.

- It is a popular fixative in perfumes to help prolong the aroma.

- Several trees produce essential oils that are sold as cedarwood, so ensure that the oil is obtained from the Cedrus atlantica.

- The wood was used for making furniture such as chests. It is very aromatic due to the high content of oils and so acts as an insect repellent.

Caution

- Avoid during pregnancy.

Cedarwood (Atlas)

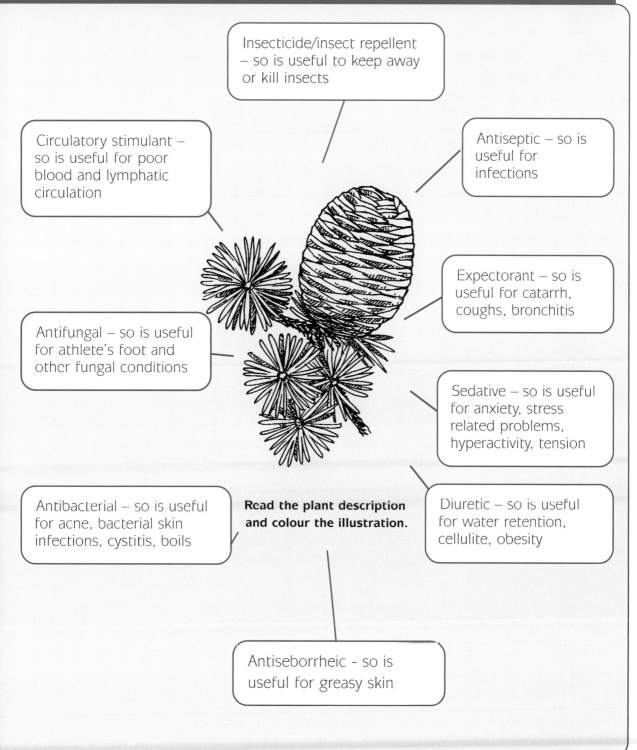

Insecticide/insect repellent – so is useful to keep away or kill insects

Circulatory stimulant – so is useful for poor blood and lymphatic circulation

Antiseptic – so is useful for infections

Antifungal – so is useful for athlete's foot and other fungal conditions

Expectorant – so is useful for catarrh, coughs, bronchitis

Sedative – so is useful for anxiety, stress related problems, hyperactivity, tension

Antibacterial – so is useful for acne, bacterial skin infections, cystitis, boils

Read the plant description and colour the illustration.

Diuretic – so is useful for water retention, cellulite, obesity

Antiseborrheic - so is useful for greasy skin

MATRICARIA RECUTITA – CHAMOMILE (GERMAN)

- **Plant description:** Herb with green leaves and daisy-like flowers (yellow head and white petals)
- **Botanical family:** Compositae
- **Note:** Middle
- **Extraction:** Steam distillation of the flowers
- **Production:** Originated in Europe and Asia. Now widely grown in many countries.
- **Blends well with:** Bergamot, carrot seed, clary sage, geranium, jasmine, lavender, patchouli, neroli, rose, rosewood, sandalwood, ylang-ylang

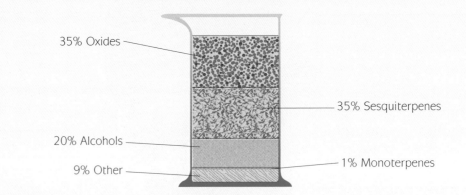

35% Oxides

35% Sesquiterpenes

20% Alcohols

9% Other

1% Monoterpenes

Notes

- There can be a slight variation from one year to the next with German chamomile because of the existence of different chemotypes.

- The oil contains a chemical called chamazulene, which gives the oil its deep blue colour.

- German chamomile is said to have liver-regenerating properties.

- The chamomile flowers smell like apples.

Chamomile (German)

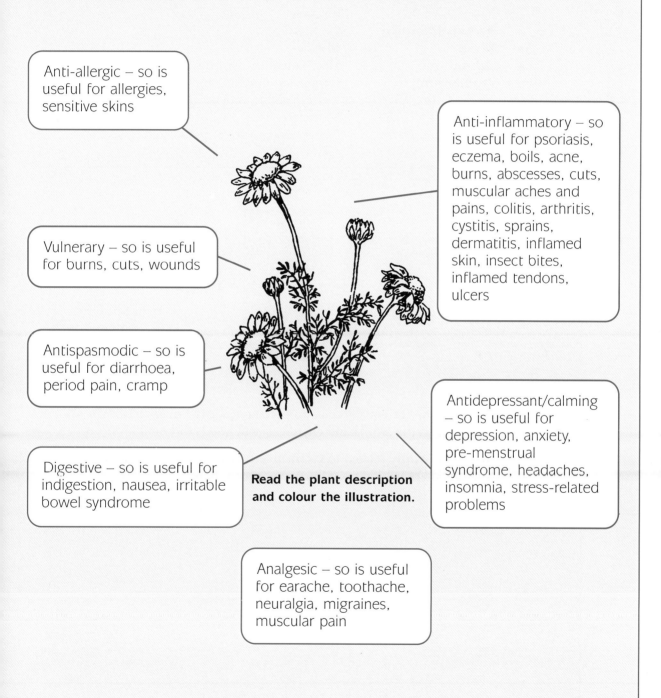

Anti-allergic – so is useful for allergies, sensitive skins

Anti-inflammatory – so is useful for psoriasis, eczema, boils, acne, burns, abscesses, cuts, muscular aches and pains, colitis, arthritis, cystitis, sprains, dermatitis, inflamed skin, insect bites, inflamed tendons, ulcers

Vulnerary – so is useful for burns, cuts, wounds

Antispasmodic – so is useful for diarrhoea, period pain, cramp

Antidepressant/calming – so is useful for depression, anxiety, pre-menstrual syndrome, headaches, insomnia, stress-related problems

Digestive – so is useful for indigestion, nausea, irritable bowel syndrome

Read the plant description and colour the illustration.

Analgesic – so is useful for earache, toothache, neuralgia, migraines, muscular pain

ORMENIS MULTICAULIS – CHAMOMILE (MAROC)

- **Plant description:** Herb with green leaves and yellow, tube-like flowers
- **Botanical family:** Compositae
- **Note:** Middle
- **Extraction:** Steam distillation of the flowers
- **Production:** Originated in Africa and southern Spain. Now widely produced. The oil is also distilled in Morocco.
- **Blends well with:** Cedarwood, cypress, frankincense, lavender, vetiver

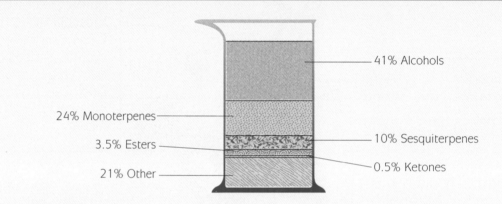

- 41% Alcohols
- 24% Monoterpenes
- 3.5% Esters
- 21% Other
- 10% Sesquiterpenes
- 0.5% Ketones

Notes

- This oil cannot be considered a replacement for German or Roman chamomile as the aroma and chemical structure is different.

- Although distantly related to German and Roman chamomile botanically, physically there is little resemblance between them.

Chamomile (Maroc)

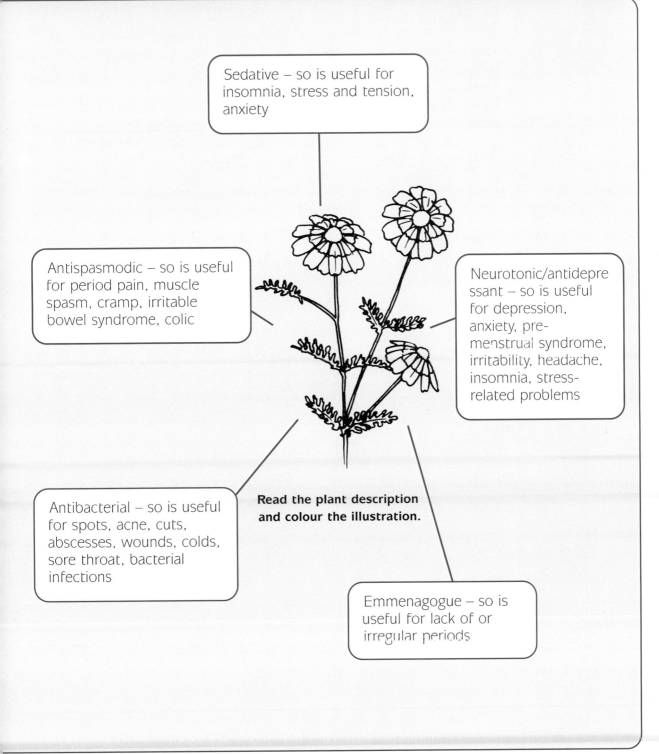

Sedative – so is useful for insomnia, stress and tension, anxiety

Antispasmodic – so is useful for period pain, muscle spasm, cramp, irritable bowel syndrome, colic

Neurotonic/antidepressant – so is useful for depression, anxiety, pre-menstrual syndrome, irritability, headache, insomnia, stress-related problems

Antibacterial – so is useful for spots, acne, cuts, abscesses, wounds, colds, sore throat, bacterial infections

Read the plant description and colour the illustration.

Emmenagogue – so is useful for lack of or irregular periods

ANTHEMIS NOBILIS – CHAMOMILE (ROMAN)

- **Plant description:** Herb with green leaves and daisy-like flowers (yellow heads and white petals). The flowers are larger than those of German chamomile.
- **Botanical family:** Compositae
- **Note:** Middle
- **Extraction:** Steam distillation of the flowers
- **Production:** Originated in Spain and western Europe. Produced in England, France, USA and Italy.
- **Blends well with:** Bergamot, clary sage, geranium, lavender, lemon, marjoram, neroli, orange, rose absolute, rose otto, rosewood, sandalwood, ylang-ylang

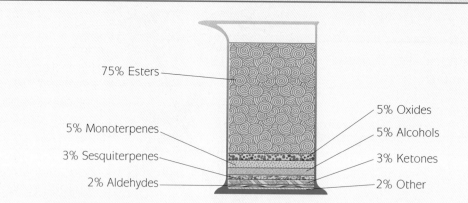

75% Esters

5% Monoterpenes

3% Sesquiterpenes

2% Aldehydes

5% Oxides

5% Alcohols

3% Ketones

2% Other

Notes

- Chamomile shampoo is used to help enhance blonde hair.
- Due to the high ester content, this oil is calming, relaxing and sedative.
- This oil is a popular choice to use on children.
- The properties and uses of chamomile often overlap with those of lavender.

Chamomile (Roman)

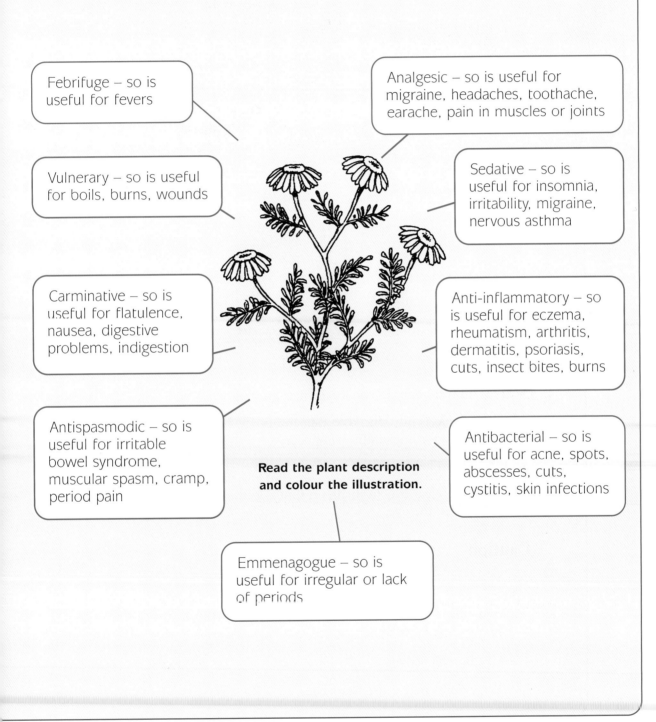

Febrifuge – so is useful for fevers

Analgesic – so is useful for migraine, headaches, toothache, earache, pain in muscles or joints

Vulnerary – so is useful for boils, burns, wounds

Sedative – so is useful for insomnia, irritability, migraine, nervous asthma

Carminative – so is useful for flatulence, nausea, digestive problems, indigestion

Anti-inflammatory – so is useful for eczema, rheumatism, arthritis, dermatitis, psoriasis, cuts, insect bites, burns

Antispasmodic – so is useful for irritable bowel syndrome, muscular spasm, cramp, period pain

Read the plant description and colour the illustration.

Antibacterial – so is useful for acne, spots, abscesses, cuts, cystitis, skin infections

Emmenagogue – so is useful for irregular or lack of periods

SALVIA SCLAREA – CLARY SAGE

- **Plant description:** Herb with large green leaves and small purple or blue flowers
- **Botanical family:** Lamiaceae
- **Note:** Top/middle
- **Extraction:** Steam distillation of the leaves and flowers
- **Production:** Originates from Russia and France
- **Blends well with:** Bergamot and other citrus oils, cypress, frankincense, geranium, jasmine, juniper, lavender, pine, sandalwood

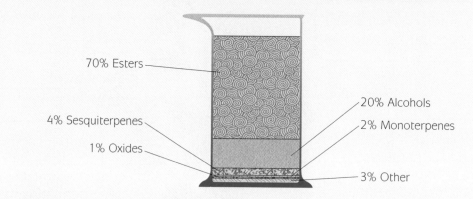

70% Esters
4% Sesquiterpenes
1% Oxides
20% Alcohols
2% Monoterpenes
3% Other

Notes

- This oil is thought to encourage hair growth.
- Clary sage was introduced to England in 1562 and was sometimes substituted for hops in brewing beer.
- It is used to help encourage labour for pregnant women.
- Known as 'clear eye' in medieval times, it was used for clearing foreign bodies from the eye.

Caution

- Do not use during pregnancy.
- Avoid use if drinking alcohol as it can increase the effects of the alcohol and may cause nightmares!
- Can be very sedative.
- Large doses may cause headaches.

Clary sage

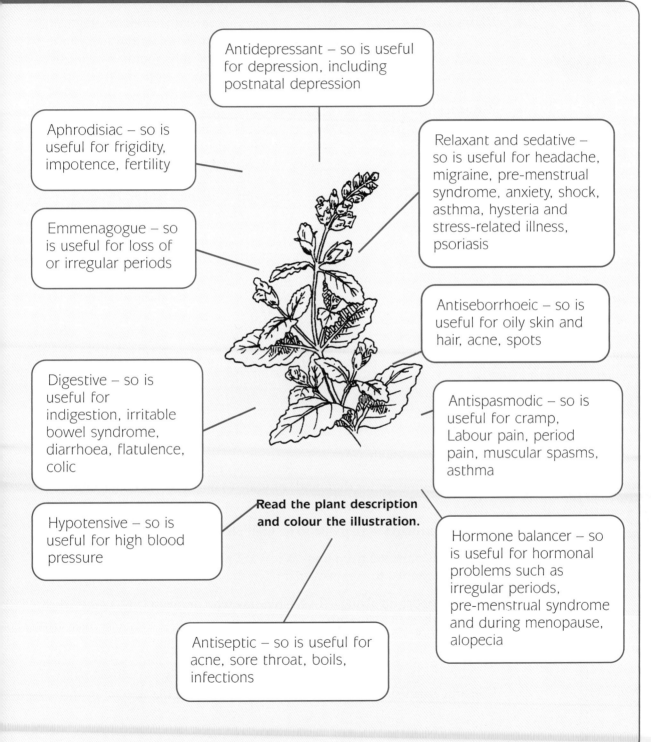

Antidepressant – so is useful for depression, including postnatal depression

Aphrodisiac – so is useful for frigidity, impotence, fertility

Relaxant and sedative – so is useful for headache, migraine, pre-menstrual syndrome, anxiety, shock, asthma, hysteria and stress-related illness, psoriasis

Emmenagogue – so is useful for loss of or irregular periods

Antiseborrhoeic – so is useful for oily skin and hair, acne, spots

Digestive – so is useful for indigestion, irritable bowel syndrome, diarrhoea, flatulence, colic

Antispasmodic – so is useful for cramp, Labour pain, period pain, muscular spasms, asthma

Read the plant description and colour the illustration.

Hypotensive – so is useful for high blood pressure

Hormone balancer – so is useful for hormonal problems such as irregular periods, pre-menstrual syndrome and during menopause, alopecia

Antiseptic – so is useful for acne, sore throat, boils, infections

SYZYGIUM AROMATICUM – CLOVE (BUD)

- **Plant description:** Slender evergreen tree with a smooth, grey trunk and large, bright green leaves. At the start of the rainy season long, pink buds appear, which turn red. These buds are beaten from the tree and dried.
- **Botanical family:** Myrtaceae
- **Note:** Base
- **Extraction:** Steam distillation of the unopened buds
- **Production:** Originated in Indonesia and Madagasgar. Now widely grown across Asia.
- **Blends well with:** Basil, black pepper, cajeput, ginger, lavender, lemon, marjoram, orange, peppermint, rosemary, thyme

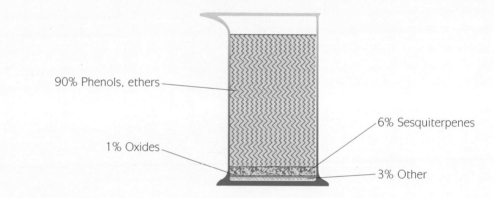

90% Phenols, ethers

6% Sesquiterpenes

1% Oxides

3% Other

Notes

- Clove has been used for thousands of years to help prevent contagious illness, especially the plague.

- Clove may irritate the skin due to its high phenol content.

- Use only oil extracted from buds as it is safer due to the lower levels of phenols (eugenols) than if extracted from the leaves or stalks.

- There is a report involving a 2-year-old boy who drank up to 10 ml of clove oil and nearly died as a result.

Caution

- Use only small amounts and with care as can irritate the skin.

Clove (bud)

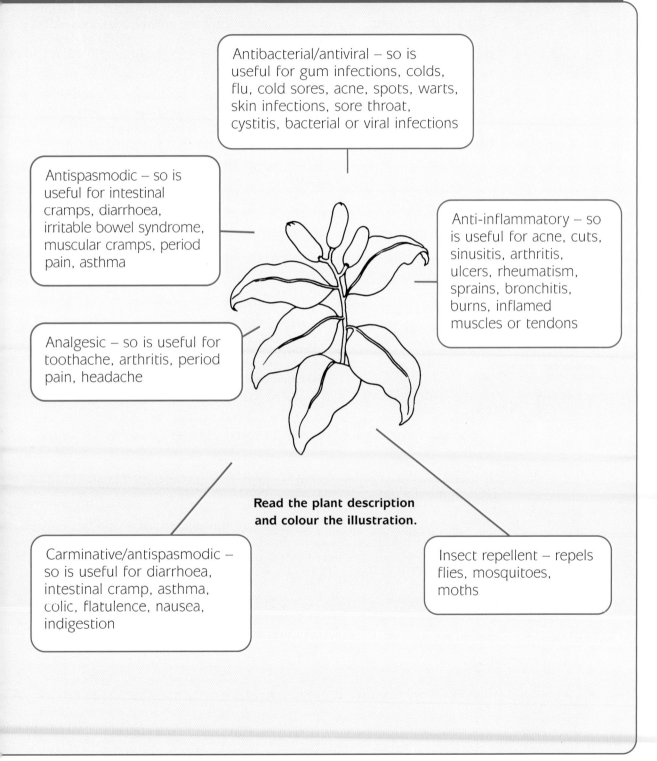

Antibacterial/antiviral – so is useful for gum infections, colds, flu, cold sores, acne, spots, warts, skin infections, sore throat, cystitis, bacterial or viral infections

Antispasmodic – so is useful for intestinal cramps, diarrhoea, irritable bowel syndrome, muscular cramps, period pain, asthma

Anti-inflammatory – so is useful for acne, cuts, sinusitis, arthritis, ulcers, rheumatism, sprains, bronchitis, burns, inflamed muscles or tendons

Analgesic – so is useful for toothache, arthritis, period pain, headache

Read the plant description and colour the illustration.

Carminative/antispasmodic – so is useful for diarrhoea, intestinal cramp, asthma, colic, flatulence, nausea, indigestion

Insect repellent – repels flies, mosquitoes, moths

CUPRESSUS SEMPERVIRENS – CYPRESS

- **Plant description:** Evergreen tree with spiky green leaves and brown, round cones
- **Botanical family:** Cupressaceae
- **Note:** Middle
- **Extraction:** Steam distillation of the leaves, flowers and twigs
- **Production:** Originates in eastern Mediterranean. Now produced in Morocco, Spain and France.
- **Blends well with:** Benzoin, bergamot, carrot, clary sage, fennel, grapefruit, juniper, lavender, lemon, orange, pine, rosemary

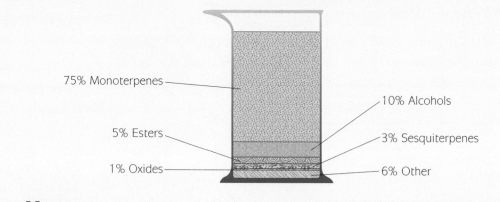

75% Monoterpenes
10% Alcohols
5% Esters
3% Sesquiterpenes
1% Oxides
6% Other

Notes

- Hippocrates recommended cypress for severe cases of haemorrhoids with bleeding!

- Dr Jean Valnet used cypress oil in hospital to treat coughing. He placed a few drops under the pillow of sufferers.

- There are many other types of cypress trees throughout the world but *Cupressus sempervirens* produces the best quality oil.

- Cypress is useful to treat very sweaty, smelly feet!

Cypress

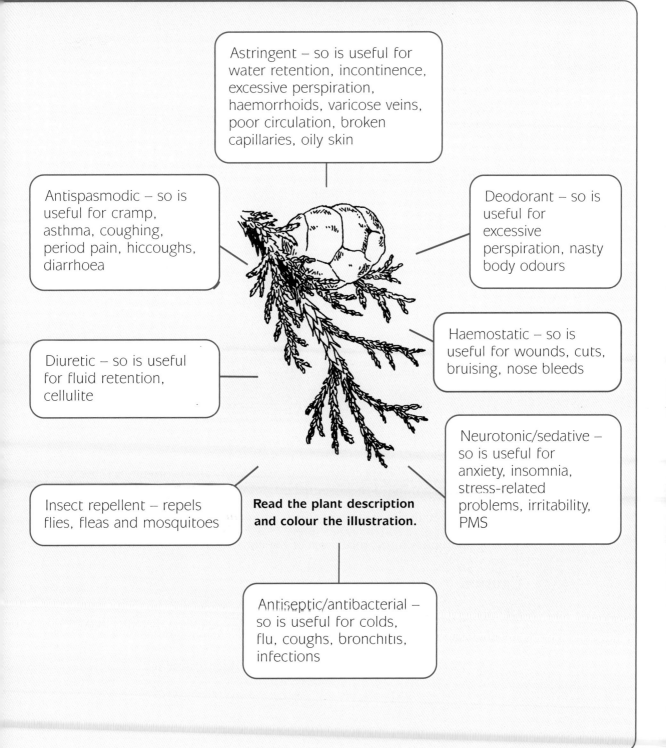

Astringent – so is useful for water retention, incontinence, excessive perspiration, haemorrhoids, varicose veins, poor circulation, broken capillaries, oily skin

Antispasmodic – so is useful for cramp, asthma, coughing, period pain, hiccoughs, diarrhoea

Deodorant – so is useful for excessive perspiration, nasty body odours

Diuretic – so is useful for fluid retention, cellulite

Haemostatic – so is useful for wounds, cuts, bruising, nose bleeds

Neurotonic/sedative – so is useful for anxiety, insomnia, stress-related problems, irritability, PMS

Insect repellent – repels flies, fleas and mosquitoes

Read the plant description and colour the illustration.

Antiseptic/antibacterial – so is useful for colds, flu, coughs, bronchitis, infections

EUCALYPTUS GLOBULUS – EUCALYPTUS (BLUE GUM)

- **Plant description:** A tall, evergreen tree. The mature tree has long, narrow, yellowish leaves and creamy/white flowers.
- **Botanical family:** Myrataceae
- **Note:** Top
- **Extraction:** Steam distillation of the leaves and twigs
- **Production:** Originated in Australia. About fifty species of eucalyptus can be found in Mediterranean countries.
- **Blends well with:** Basil, cajeput, cedarwood, frankincense, ginger, juniper, lavender, lemon, marjoram, peppermint, pine, rosemary, tea tree and thyme

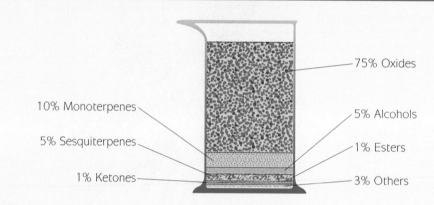

- 75% Oxides
- 5% Alcohols
- 1% Esters
- 3% Others
- 10% Monoterpenes
- 5% Sesquiterpenes
- 1% Ketones

Notes

- There are over 700 species of eucalyptus! Only about fifteen of these species are used to produced the essential oil.

- Due to its high oxide content this oil is stimulating and warming.

- The aborigines burnt the leaves of the eucalyptus to relieve fever.

Caution

- Applied externally this oil is safe but is highly toxic if swallowed; it can damage the liver or even cause death.

- Do not use in conjunction with homeopathic treatment.

Eucalyptus (blue gum)

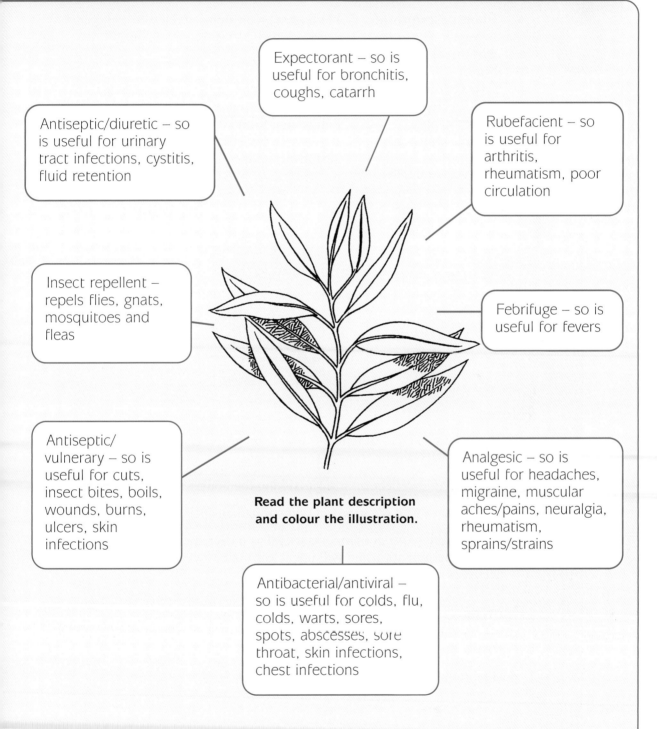

Expectorant – so is useful for bronchitis, coughs, catarrh

Antiseptic/diuretic – so is useful for urinary tract infections, cystitis, fluid retention

Rubefacient – so is useful for arthritis, rheumatism, poor circulation

Insect repellent – repels flies, gnats, mosquitoes and fleas

Febrifuge – so is useful for fevers

Antiseptic/ vulnerary – so is useful for cuts, insect bites, boils, wounds, burns, ulcers, skin infections

Read the plant description and colour the illustration.

Analgesic – so is useful for headaches, migraine, muscular aches/pains, neuralgia, rheumatism, sprains/strains

Antibacterial/antiviral – so is useful for colds, flu, colds, warts, sores, spots, abscesses, sore throat, skin infections, chest infections

FOENICULUM VULGARE – FENNEL (SWEET)

- **Plant description:** Herb with green stems and leaves and golden yellow flowers
- **Botanical family:** Umbelliferae
- **Note:** Middle
- **Extraction:** Steam distillation of the crushed seeds
- **Production:** Grows wild in many countries such as France and Italy. Often found near the sea.
- **Blends well with:** Basil, carrot, clary sage, cypress, geranium, grapefruit, juniper, lavender, lemon, peppermint, rose, rosemary and sandalwood

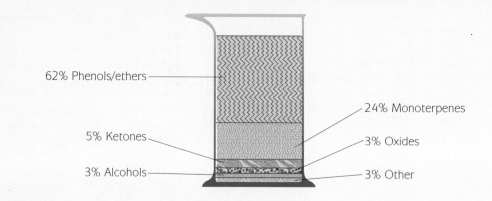

62% Phenols/ethers
5% Ketones
3% Alcohols
24% Monoterpenes
3% Oxides
3% Other

Notes

- There are two types of fennel – sweet and bitter. Use sweet fennel as bitter fennel, causes sensitisation in some people.

- Fennel is an excellent oil for detoxifying the body.

- Fennel tea can aid constipation as it strengthens peristalsis.

- If trying to lose weight fennel is useful as it decreases the appetite, helps get rid of water retention and will help clear toxins away from fat, so also decreases cellulite.

Caution

- Avoid during pregnancy.

- Do not use on epileptics.

Fennel (sweet)

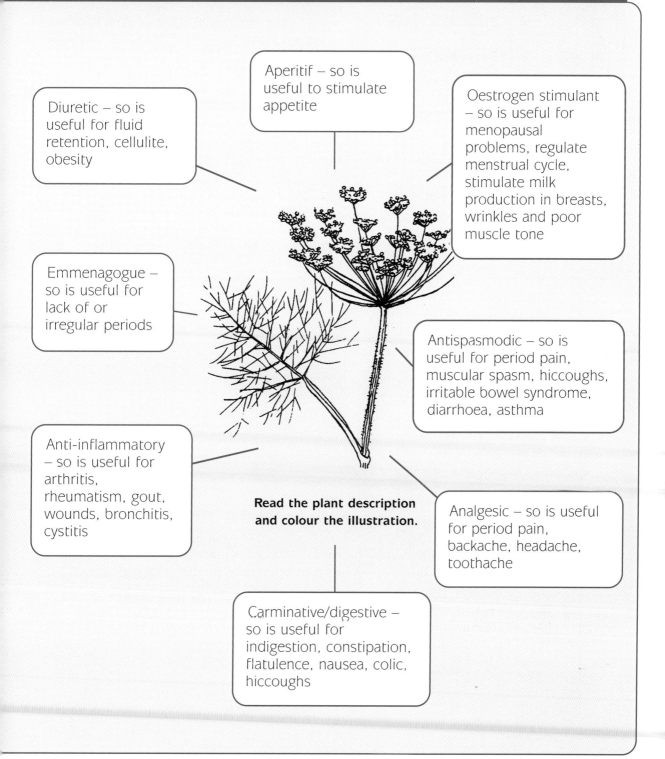

Aperitif – so is useful to stimulate appetite

Diuretic – so is useful for fluid retention, cellulite, obesity

Oestrogen stimulant – so is useful for menopausal problems, regulate menstrual cycle, stimulate milk production in breasts, wrinkles and poor muscle tone

Emmenagogue – so is useful for lack of or irregular periods

Antispasmodic – so is useful for period pain, muscular spasm, hiccoughs, irritable bowel syndrome, diarrhoea, asthma

Anti-inflammatory – so is useful for arthritis, rheumatism, gout, wounds, bronchitis, cystitis

Read the plant description and colour the illustration.

Analgesic – so is useful for period pain, backache, headache, toothache

Carminative/digestive – so is useful for indigestion, constipation, flatulence, nausea, colic, hiccoughs

BOSWELLIA CARTERI – FRANKINCENSE

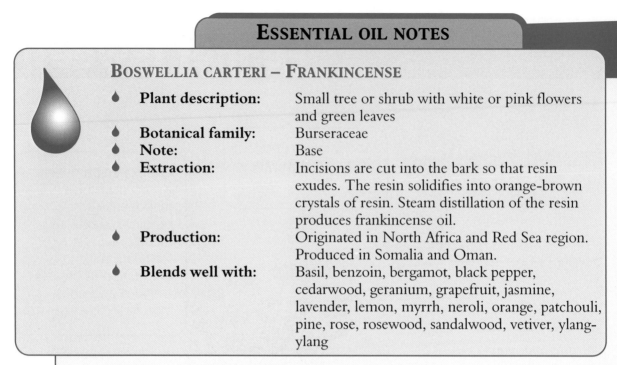

- **Plant description:** Small tree or shrub with white or pink flowers and green leaves
- **Botanical family:** Burseraceae
- **Note:** Base
- **Extraction:** Incisions are cut into the bark so that resin exudes. The resin solidifies into orange-brown crystals of resin. Steam distillation of the resin produces frankincense oil.
- **Production:** Originated in North Africa and Red Sea region. Produced in Somalia and Oman.
- **Blends well with:** Basil, benzoin, bergamot, black pepper, cedarwood, geranium, grapefruit, jasmine, lavender, lemon, myrrh, neroli, orange, patchouli, pine, rose, rosewood, sandalwood, vetiver, ylang-ylang

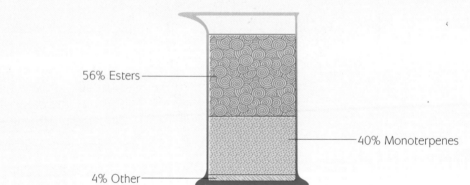

56% Esters
40% Monoterpenes
4% Other

Notes

- Frankincense is also known as olibanum.

- This oil has been used for over 5000 years, originally as incense by many cultures because it slows down breathing and produces feelings of calm.

- The Egyptians used frankincense when embalming their dead.

- It is useful for older skin types for its tonic effects on the skin, as it helps to restore tone and slow down appearance of wrinkles.

Frankincense

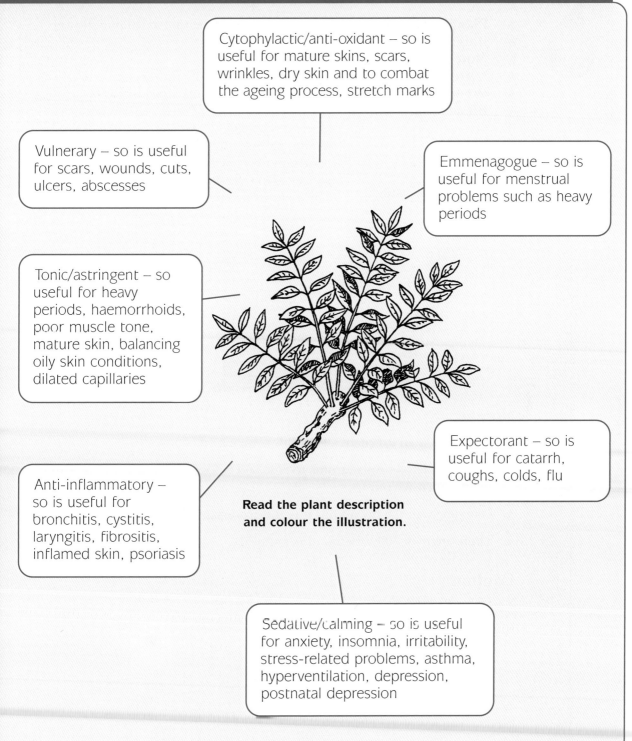

Cytophylactic/anti-oxidant – so is useful for mature skins, scars, wrinkles, dry skin and to combat the ageing process, stretch marks

Vulnerary – so is useful for scars, wounds, cuts, ulcers, abscesses

Emmenagogue – so is useful for menstrual problems such as heavy periods

Tonic/astringent – so useful for heavy periods, haemorrhoids, poor muscle tone, mature skin, balancing oily skin conditions, dilated capillaries

Expectorant – so is useful for catarrh, coughs, colds, flu

Anti-inflammatory – so is useful for bronchitis, cystitis, laryngitis, fibrositis, inflamed skin, psoriasis

Read the plant description and colour the illustration.

Sedative/calming – so is useful for anxiety, insomnia, irritability, stress-related problems, asthma, hyperventilation, depression, postnatal depression

PELARGONIUM GRAVEOLENS – GERANIUM

- **Plant description:** Plant with green leaves and small pink flowers
- **Botanical family:** Geraniaceae
- **Note:** Middle
- **Extraction:** Steam distillation of the flowers, stalks and leaves
- **Production:** China and Egypt are main producers
- **Blends well with:** Basil, bergamot, carrot seed, cedarwood, clary sage, frankincense, grapefruit, jasmine, lavender, lemon, melissa, neroli, orange, patchouli, petitgrain, rose, rosemary, rosewood, sandalwood, vetiver, ylang-ylang

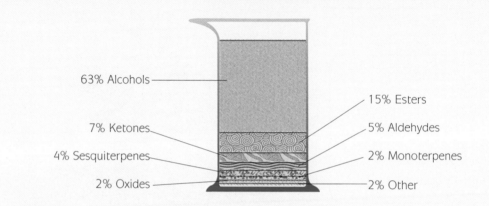

63% Alcohols
15% Esters
7% Ketones
5% Aldehydes
4% Sesquiterpenes
2% Monoterpenes
2% Oxides
2% Other

Notes

- Geranium is an excellent all-round women's oil.

- Geranium has a similar aroma to rose and is sometimes added to it as rose is a very expensive oil.

- Like nearly all the flower oils it is antidepressant and antiseptic.

- There are over 700 varieties of geranium!

Caution

- May irritate sensitive skins.

Geranium

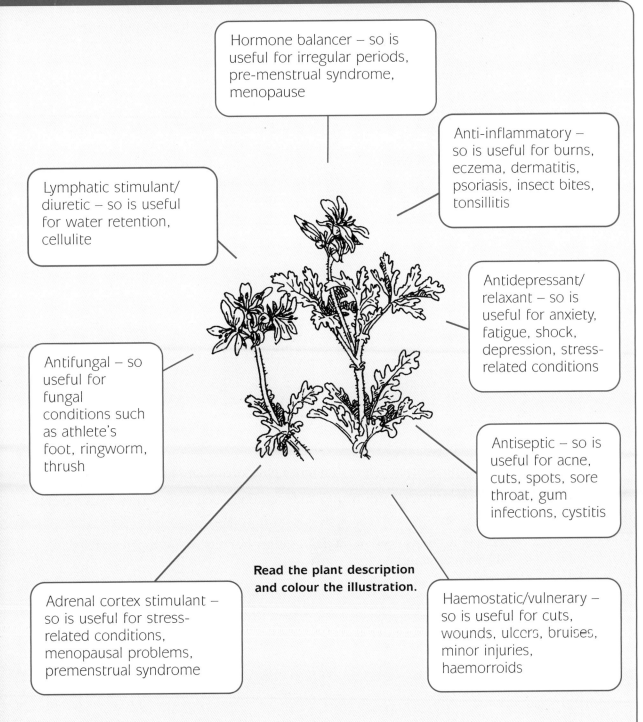

Hormone balancer – so is useful for irregular periods, pre-menstrual syndrome, menopause

Anti-inflammatory – so is useful for burns, eczema, dermatitis, psoriasis, insect bites, tonsillitis

Lymphatic stimulant/ diuretic – so is useful for water retention, cellulite

Antidepressant/ relaxant – so is useful for anxiety, fatigue, shock, depression, stress-related conditions

Antifungal – so useful for fungal conditions such as athlete's foot, ringworm, thrush

Antiseptic – so is useful for acne, cuts, spots, sore throat, gum infections, cystitis

Read the plant description and colour the illustration.

Adrenal cortex stimulant – so is useful for stress-related conditions, menopausal problems, premenstrual syndrome

Haemostatic/vulnerary – so is useful for cuts, wounds, ulcers, bruises, minor injuries, haemorroids

ZINGIBER OFFICINALE – GINGER

- **Plant description:** Herb with brown/greyish roots and narrow, spear-shaped green leaves. It also bears white or yellow flowers.
- **Botanical family:** Zingiberaceae
- **Note:** Top
- **Extraction:** Steam distillation of the root
- **Production:** Originated in India and China. Now widely grown and produced.
- **Blends well with:** Black pepper, cajeput, cedarwood, clove, eucalyptus, frankincense, geranium, grapefruit, lemon, orange, peppermint, rosemary, tea tree, thyme

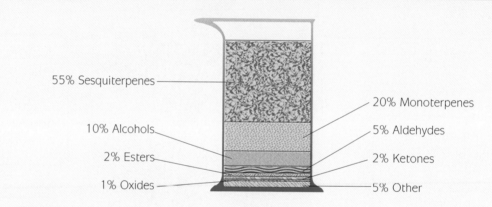

55% Sesquiterpenes
20% Monoterpenes
10% Alcohols
5% Aldehydes
2% Esters
2% Ketones
1% Oxides
5% Other

Notes

- The Chinese used ginger to remove phlegm and strengthen the heart.
- It is a good remedy for nausea and vomiting, such as associated with travel sickness.
- Ginger is often added to food, i.e. ginger biscuits, and is excellent for the digestive system.

Caution

- May irritate sensitive skins.

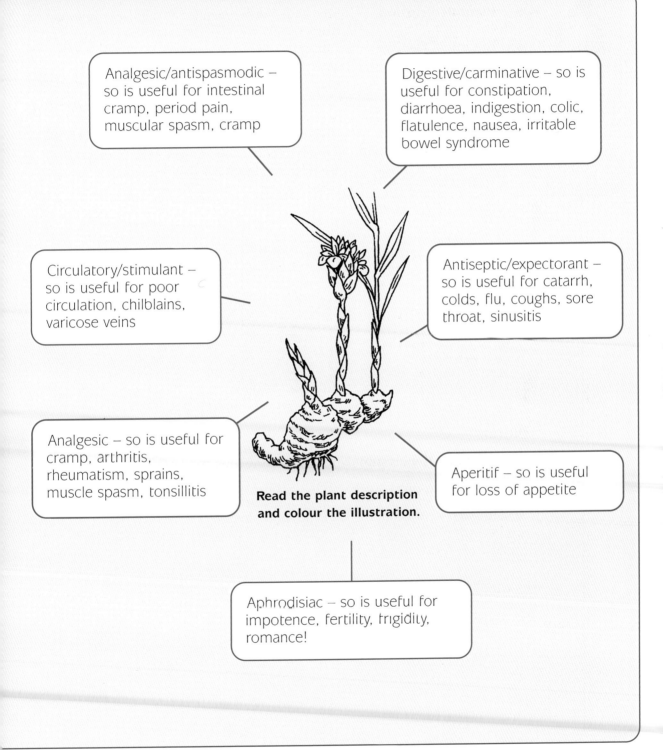

Analgesic/antispasmodic – so is useful for intestinal cramp, period pain, muscular spasm, cramp

Digestive/carminative – so is useful for constipation, diarrhoea, indigestion, colic, flatulence, nausea, irritable bowel syndrome

Circulatory/stimulant – so is useful for poor circulation, chilblains, varicose veins

Antiseptic/expectorant – so is useful for catarrh, colds, flu, coughs, sore throat, sinusitis

Analgesic – so is useful for cramp, arthritis, rheumatism, sprains, muscle spasm, tonsillitis

Read the plant description and colour the illustration.

Aperitif – so is useful for loss of appetite

Aphrodisiac – so is useful for impotence, fertility, frigidity, romance!

CITRUS X PARADISI – GRAPEFRUIT

- **Plant description:** Tree with glossy green leaves and large yellow fruits
- **Botanical family:** Rutaceae
- **Note:** Top
- **Extraction:** Expressed from the peel of the fruit
- **Production:** Originated in Asia and West Indies. Now grown in many countries.
- **Blends well with:** Basil, bergamot, carrot seed, cedarwood, cypress, fennel, frankincense, juniper, geranium, ginger, lavender, orange, rosemary, rosewood, vetiver, ylang-ylang

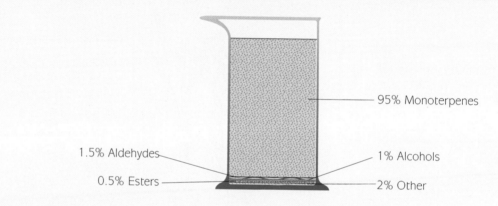

95% Monoterpenes

1.5% Aldehydes

0.5% Esters

1% Alcohols

2% Other

Notes

- This essential oil is stimulating, due to the high content of monoterpenes.
- Grapefruit oxidises quickly so has a short shelf life.
- Although a citrus oil, this oil is not phototoxic.

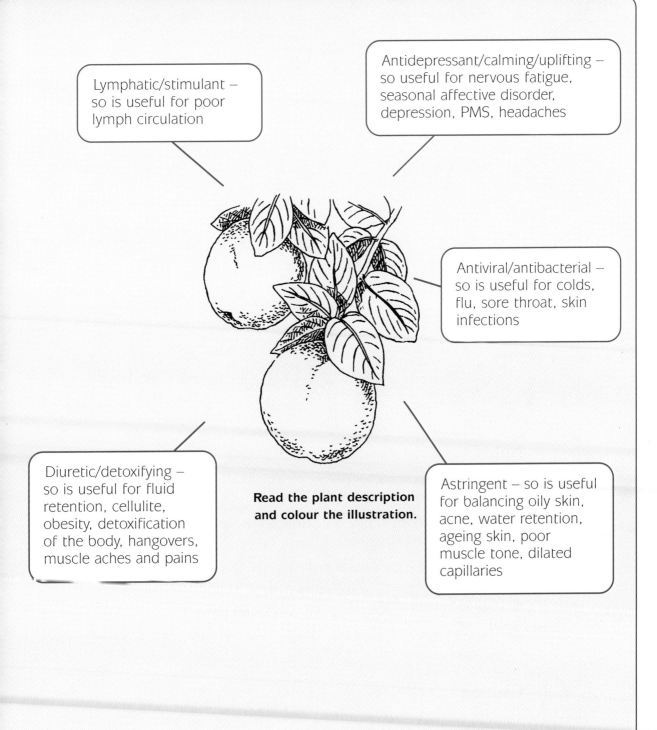

Lymphatic/stimulant – so is useful for poor lymph circulation

Antidepressant/calming/uplifting – so useful for nervous fatigue, seasonal affective disorder, depression, PMS, headaches

Antiviral/antibacterial – so is useful for colds, flu, sore throat, skin infections

Diuretic/detoxifying – so is useful for fluid retention, cellulite, obesity, detoxification of the body, hangovers, muscle aches and pains

Read the plant description and colour the illustration.

Astringent – so is useful for balancing oily skin, acne, water retention, ageing skin, poor muscle tone, dilated capillaries

ESSENTIAL OIL NOTES

JASMINUM OFFICINALE – JASMINE

- **Plant description:** Evergreen shrub with bright green leaves and star-shaped, white flowers
- **Botanical family:** Oleaceae
- **Note:** Base
- **Extraction:** CO_2 method, enfleurage or solvent extraction of the flowers. An absolute is produced by steam distillation.
- **Production:** Originated in China and India. Also produced in France, Italy, Morocco and Egypt.
- **Blends well with:** Bergamot, cedarwood, clary sage, frankincense, geranium, lavender, melissa, neroli, orange, rose, rosewood, sandalwood, ylang-ylang. It will blend well with virtually any other oil.

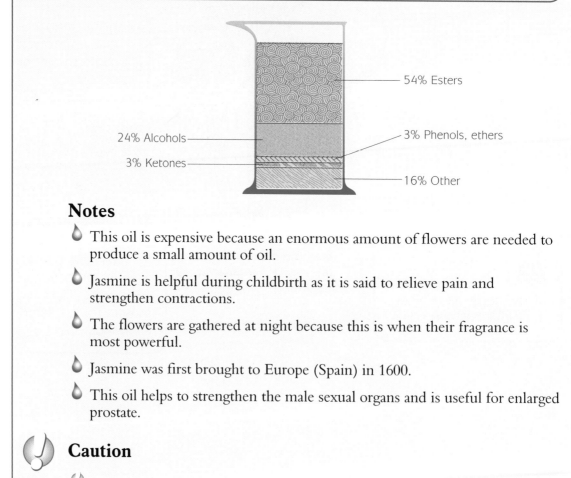

- 54% Esters
- 24% Alcohols
- 3% Phenols, ethers
- 3% Ketones
- 16% Other

Notes

- This oil is expensive because an enormous amount of flowers are needed to produce a small amount of oil.
- Jasmine is helpful during childbirth as it is said to relieve pain and strengthen contractions.
- The flowers are gathered at night because this is when their fragrance is most powerful.
- Jasmine was first brought to Europe (Spain) in 1600.
- This oil helps to strengthen the male sexual organs and is useful for enlarged prostate.

Caution

- Avoid during pregnancy.

Aromatherapy for Holistic Therapists

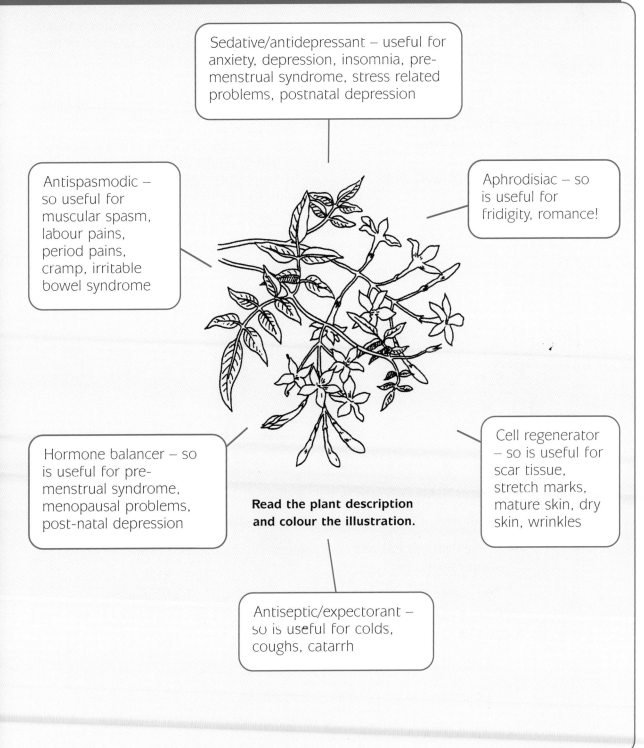

Sedative/antidepressant – useful for anxiety, depression, insomnia, pre-menstrual syndrome, stress related problems, postnatal depression

Aphrodisiac – so is useful for fridigity, romance!

Antispasmodic – so useful for muscular spasm, labour pains, period pains, cramp, irritable bowel syndrome

Hormone balancer – so is useful for pre-menstrual syndrome, menopausal problems, post-natal depression

Read the plant description and colour the illustration.

Cell regenerator – so is useful for scar tissue, stretch marks, mature skin, dry skin, wrinkles

Antiseptic/expectorant – so is useful for colds, coughs, catarrh

JUNIPERUS COMMUNIS – JUNIPER

- **Plant description:** Evergreen shrub with spiky green leaves, small flowers and little berries, which are green in the first year, turning black in the second and third year
- **Botanical family:** Cupressaceae
- **Note:** Middle
- **Extraction:** Steam distillation of the berries
- **Production:** Originated in France, Italy, Canada, Scandinavia and now widely produced, especially in Europe
- **Blends well with:** Benzoin, bergamot, cedarwood, cypress, fennel, frankincense, geranium, grapefruit, orange, lavender, lemon, lemongrass, rosemary, sandalwood

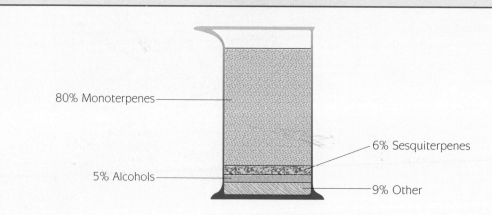

80% Monoterpenes

6% Sesquiterpenes

5% Alcohols

9% Other

Notes

- Juniper berries are used in the production of gin.
- An inferior oil is produced from the leaves and twigs.
- In the fifteenth and sixteenth centuries herbalists used juniper to protect against the plague.
- The most important benefit of juniper is its detoxifying property.

Caution

- Avoid during pregnancy.
- Do not use on people with kidney disease.

Juniper

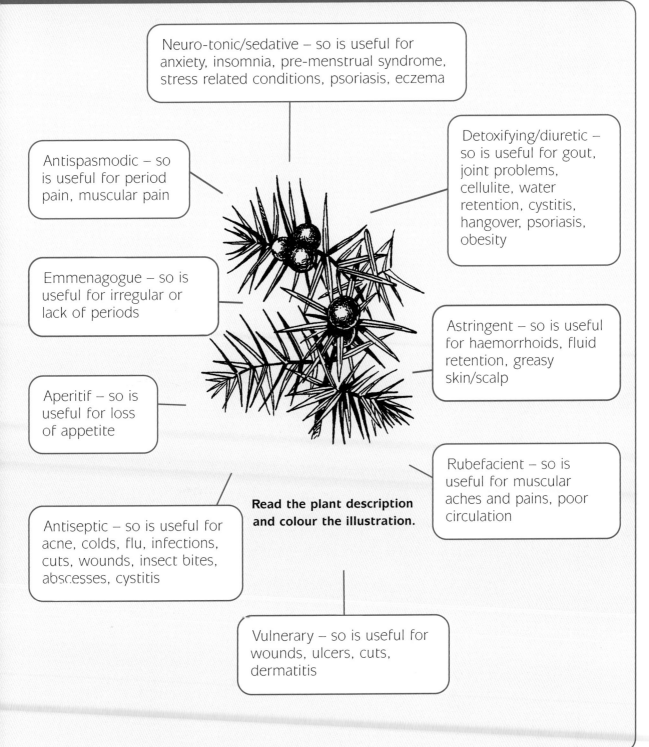

Neuro-tonic/sedative – so is useful for anxiety, insomnia, pre-menstrual syndrome, stress related conditions, psoriasis, eczema

Detoxifying/diuretic – so is useful for gout, joint problems, cellulite, water retention, cystitis, hangover, psoriasis, obesity

Antispasmodic – so is useful for period pain, muscular pain

Emmenagogue – so is useful for irregular or lack of periods

Astringent – so is useful for haemorrhoids, fluid retention, greasy skin/scalp

Aperitif – so is useful for loss of appetite

Rubefacient – so is useful for muscular aches and pains, poor circulation

Read the plant description and colour the illustration.

Antiseptic – so is useful for acne, colds, flu, infections, cuts, wounds, insect bites, abscesses, cystitis

Vulnerary – so is useful for wounds, ulcers, cuts, dermatitis

LAVENDULA ANGUSTIFOLIA – LAVENDER

- **Plant description:** An evergreen woody shrub with green narrow leaves and violet blue flowers
- **Botanical family:** Lamiaceae
- **Note:** Middle
- **Extraction:** Steam distillation of the flowers and stems
- **Production:** Originated in the mountainous regions of the Mediterranean. Now grown in many countries such as England and France.
- **Blends well with:** Benzoin, bergamot, chamomile, clary sage, geranium, jasmine, lemon, orange, patchouli, pine, thyme, rosemary, rosewood, ylang-ylang. Blends well with nearly all oils!

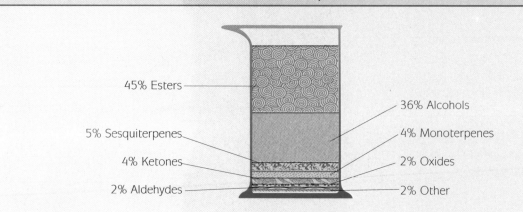

45% Esters
5% Sesquiterpenes
4% Ketones
2% Aldehydes
36% Alcohols
4% Monoterpenes
2% Oxides
2% Other

Notes

○ Lavender can be applied neat to the skin.

○ When blended with other oils lavender increases their therapeutic effects.

○ When grown at high altitudes more esters are produced.

○ There is no need to use pesticide when growing lavender as it is a natural insecticide.

Lavender

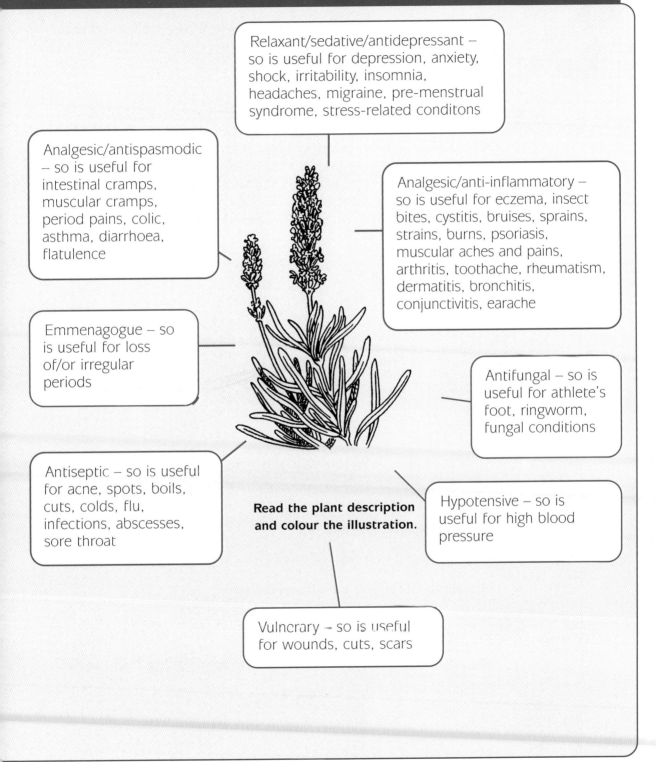

Relaxant/sedative/antidepressant – so is useful for depression, anxiety, shock, irritability, insomnia, headaches, migraine, pre-menstrual syndrome, stress-related conditons

Analgesic/antispasmodic – so is useful for intestinal cramps, muscular cramps, period pains, colic, asthma, diarrhoea, flatulence

Analgesic/anti-inflammatory – so is useful for eczema, insect bites, cystitis, bruises, sprains, strains, burns, psoriasis, muscular aches and pains, arthritis, toothache, rheumatism, dermatitis, bronchitis, conjunctivitis, earache

Emmenagogue – so is useful for loss of/or irregular periods

Antifungal – so is useful for athlete's foot, ringworm, fungal conditions

Antiseptic – so is useful for acne, spots, boils, cuts, colds, flu, infections, abscesses, sore throat

Read the plant description and colour the illustration.

Hypotensive – so is useful for high blood pressure

Vulncrary – so is useful for wounds, cuts, scars

CITRUS LIMON – LEMON

- **Plant description:** Small evergreen tree with green leaves, bearing yellow fruits
- **Botanical family:** Rutaceae
- **Note:** Top
- **Extraction:** Expression of the peel of the fruit
- **Production:** Originated in India but now widely grown. Found throughout the Mediterranean and in California.
- **Blends well with:** Benzoin, bergamot, cedarwood, clove, eucalyptus, fennel, frankincense, ginger, juniper, lavender, lemongrass, mandarin, neroli, rose, rosemary, sandalwood, ylang-ylang

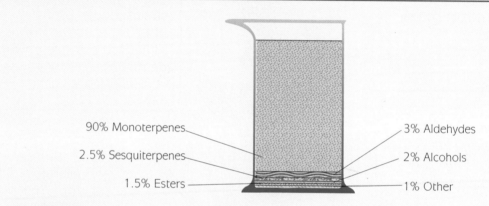

90% Monoterpenes

2.5% Sesquiterpenes

1.5% Esters

3% Aldehydes

2% Alcohols

1% Other

Notes

- It takes as many as 3,000 lemons to produce a kilogram of oil.
- Lemon is one of the most vitamin rich oils containing vitamins A, B and C.
- It is understandable why lemon is added to cold and flu remedies, considering its beneficial properties.
- Research in Japan has found that lemon can help improve concentration!
- There are about forty-seven varieties of lemon.

Caution

- May cause irritation to the skin so needs to be well diluted with carrier.
- Phototoxic so avoid direct sunlight.

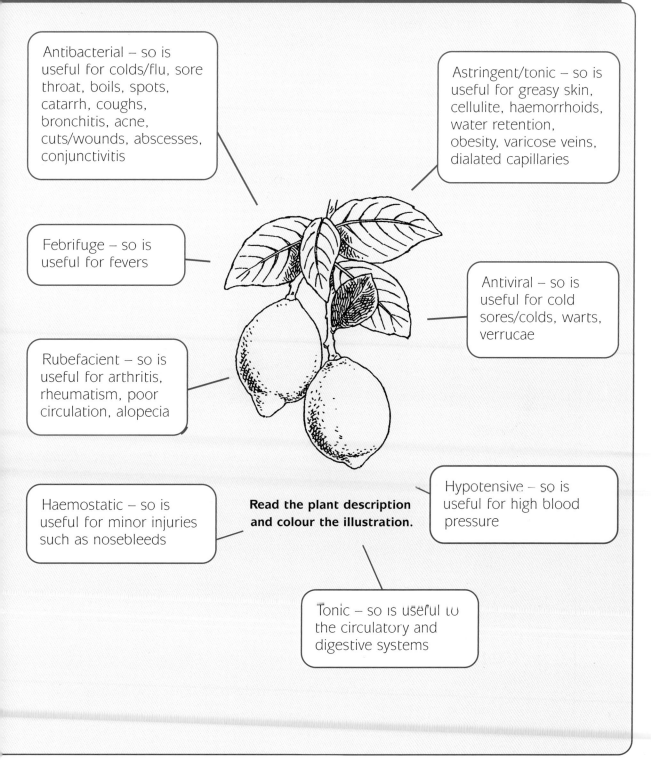

Antibacterial – so is useful for colds/flu, sore throat, boils, spots, catarrh, coughs, bronchitis, acne, cuts/wounds, abscesses, conjunctivitis

Astringent/tonic – so is useful for greasy skin, cellulite, haemorrhoids, water retention, obesity, varicose veins, dialated capillaries

Febrifuge – so is useful for fevers

Antiviral – so is useful for cold sores/colds, warts, verrucae

Rubefacient – so is useful for arthritis, rheumatism, poor circulation, alopecia

Haemostatic – so is useful for minor injuries such as nosebleeds

Read the plant description and colour the illustration.

Hypotensive – so is useful for high blood pressure

Tonic – so is useful to the circulatory and digestive systems

CYMBOPOGON CITRATUS – LEMONGRASS

- **Plant description:** Tall, fast growing, yellow/green-coloured aromatic grass
- **Botanical family:** Gramineae
- **Note:** Top
- **Extraction:** The grass is finely chopped and then steam distilled
- **Production:** Originated in India, now cultivated mainly in Africa, West Indies and tropical Asia
- **Blends well with:** Basil, bergamot, cedarwood, geranium, grapefruit, lavender, lemon, melissa, petitgrain, rosemary, tea tree, vetiver

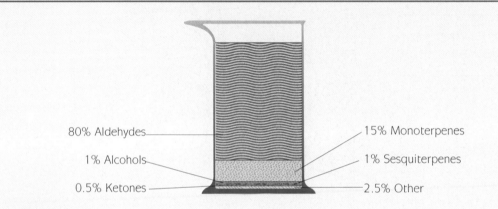

80% Aldehydes   15% Monoterpenes

1% Alcohols   1% Sesquiterpenes

0.5% Ketones   2.5% Other

Notes

- In India lemongrass was traditionally used to help treat fevers and infectious illness.
- All lemon-scented oils are a good insect repellent and are useful to protect animals from fleas and ticks.
- Research in India has shown that lemongrass acts as a sedative on the central nervous system.
- This oil is sometimes used to adulterate more expensive oils, such as melissa.
- Due to the high aldehyde content this oil is sedative, calming and relaxing.

Caution

Can cause irritation or sensitisation to the skin so needs to be used well diluted.

Lemongrass

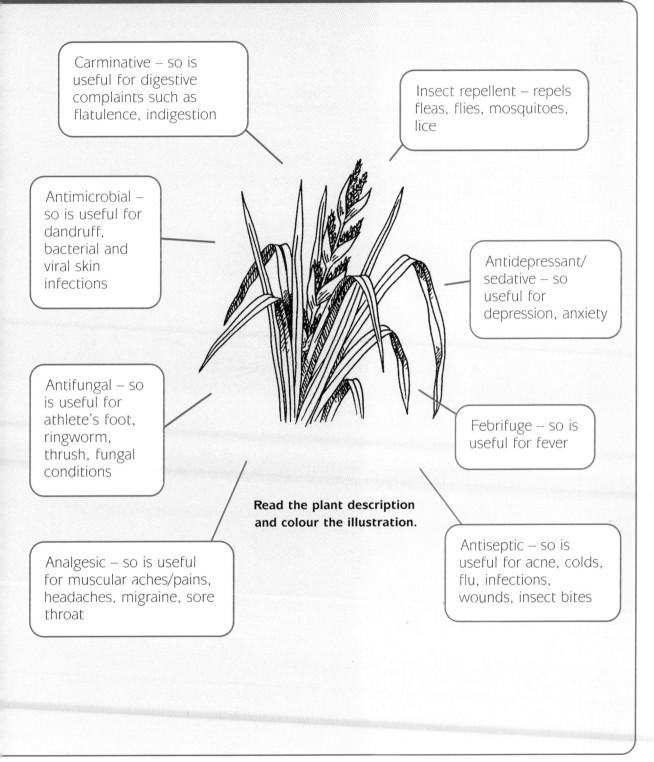

Carminative – so is useful for digestive complaints such as flatulence, indigestion

Insect repellent – repels fleas, flies, mosquitoes, lice

Antimicrobial – so is useful for dandruff, bacterial and viral skin infections

Antidepressant/ sedative – so useful for depression, anxiety

Antifungal – so is useful for athlete's foot, ringworm, thrush, fungal conditions

Febrifuge – so is useful for fever

Read the plant description and colour the illustration.

Analgesic – so is useful for muscular aches/pains, headaches, migraine, sore throat

Antiseptic – so is useful for acne, colds, flu, infections, wounds, insect bites

CITRUS RETICULATA – MANDARIN

- **Plant description:** Tree with green leaves, bearing orange fruit
- **Botanical family:** Rutaceae
- **Note:** Top
- **Extraction:** Expression of the peel of fruit
- **Production:** Originated in China. Now widely cultivated.
- **Blends well with:** Bergamot, black pepper, chamomile (Roman and German), clove, grapefruit, jasmine, lavender, lemon, marjoram, neroli, orange, petitgrain, rose, sandalwood, ylang-ylang

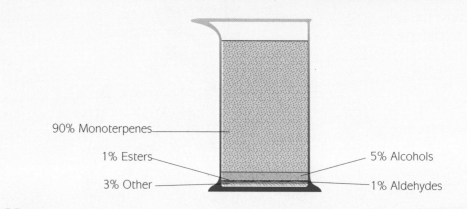

90% Monoterpenes

1% Esters

3% Other

5% Alcohols

1% Aldehydes

Notes

- Mandarin is a gentle oil so is ideal to use on children, pregnant women and elderly people.

- This fruit was named mandarin as it was a traditional gift to the mandarins (public officials) of China.

- This oil is often used in combination with neroli and wheatgerm oil to help prevent stretch marks during pregnancy.

Mandarin

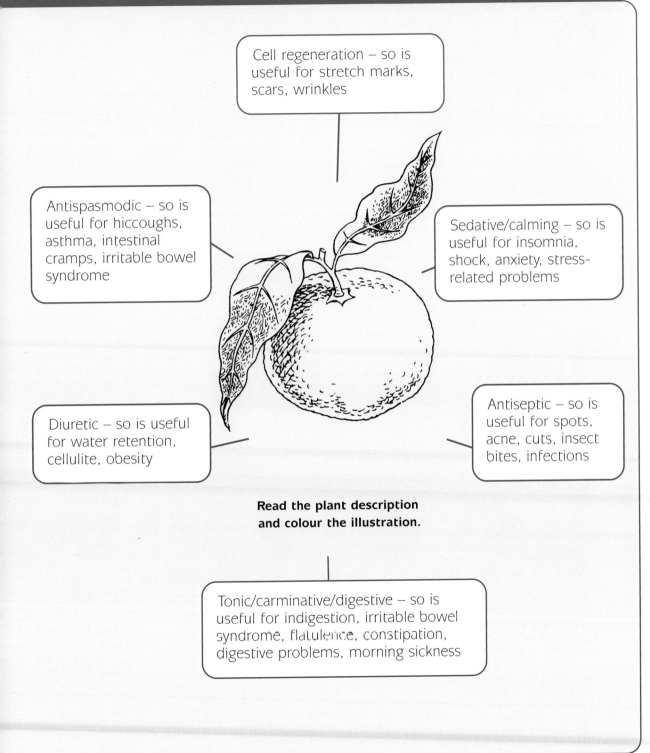

Cell regeneration – so is useful for stretch marks, scars, wrinkles

Antispasmodic – so is useful for hiccoughs, asthma, intestinal cramps, irritable bowel syndrome

Sedative/calming – so is useful for insomnia, shock, anxiety, stress-related problems

Diuretic – so is useful for water retention, cellulite, obesity

Antiseptic – so is useful for spots, acne, cuts, insect bites, infections

Read the plant description and colour the illustration.

Tonic/carminative/digestive – so is useful for indigestion, irritable bowel syndrome, flatulence, constipation, digestive problems, morning sickness

ORIGANUM MARJORANA – MARJORAM (SWEET)

- **Plant description:** Herb with dark green oval leaves and clusters of small white flowers
- **Botanical family:** Lamiaceae
- **Note:** Middle
- **Extraction:** Steam distillation of the whole plant
- **Production:** Originated in Mediterranean region, North Africa and Egypt. Produced in France, Egypt and Tunisia.
- **Blends well with:** Bergamot, cedarwood, chamomile, clove, cypress, lavender, mandarin, orange, rosemary, rosewood, ylang-ylang

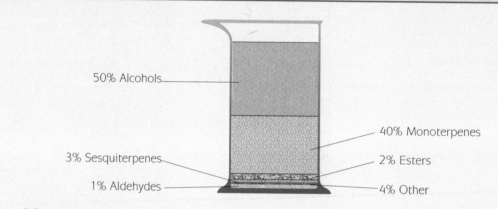

50% Alcohols

3% Sesquiterpenes

1% Aldehydes

40% Monoterpenes

2% Esters

4% Other

Notes

- Sweet marjoram should not be confused with Spanish marjoram, which actually belongs to the thyme species.

- Marjoram is a useful oil to use at times of grief.

- Like most of the Labitae family it will grow almost anywhere, and is often seen in English gardens.

- Marjoram is reputed to be an anti-aphrodisiac, so useful for people who wish to be celibate!

Caution

- Do not use during pregnancy.

Marjoram (sweet)

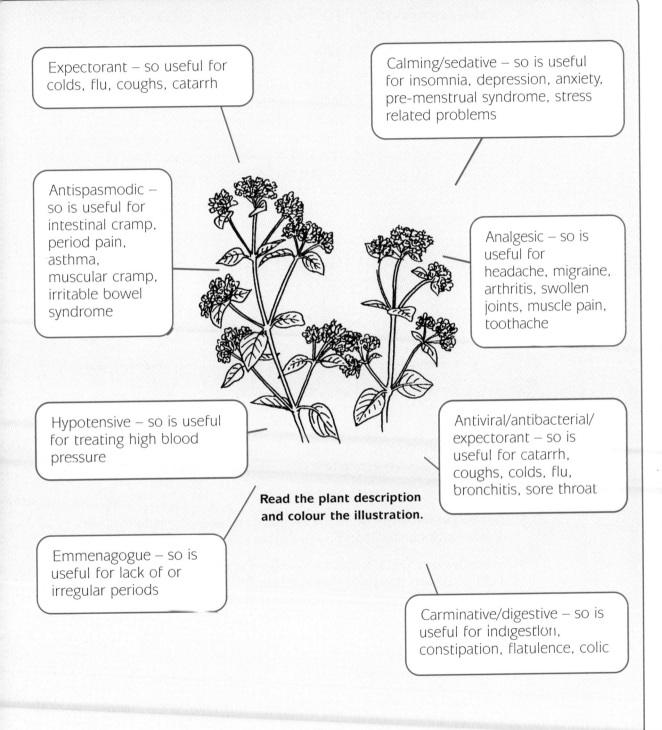

Expectorant – so useful for colds, flu, coughs, catarrh

Calming/sedative – so is useful for insomnia, depression, anxiety, pre-menstrual syndrome, stress related problems

Antispasmodic – so is useful for intestinal cramp, period pain, asthma, muscular cramp, irritable bowel syndrome

Analgesic – so is useful for headache, migraine, arthritis, swollen joints, muscle pain, toothache

Hypotensive – so is useful for treating high blood pressure

Antiviral/antibacterial/expectorant – so is useful for catarrh, coughs, colds, flu, bronchitis, sore throat

Read the plant description and colour the illustration.

Emmenagogue – so is useful for lack of or irregular periods

Carminative/digestive – so is useful for indigestion, constipation, flatulence, colic

MELISSA OFFICINALIS – MELISSA

- **Plant description:** Herb with green leaves and tiny white or pink flowers
- **Botanical family:** Lamiaceae
- **Note:** Middle
- **Extraction:** Steam distillation of the leaves and flowering tops
- **Production:** Originated in Mediterranean region. Produced in France, Wales, Ireland and Germany.
- **Blends well with:** Bergamot, cedarwood, geranium, jasmine, lavender, lemon, lemongrass, neroli, rose, sweet marjoram, ylang-ylang. Blends well with floral and citrus oils

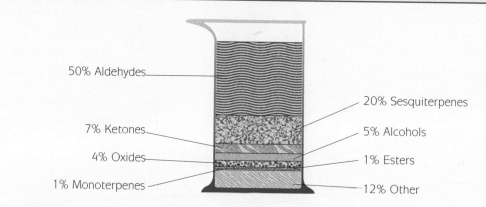

50% Aldehydes

7% Ketones

4% Oxides

1% Monoterpenes

20% Sesquiterpenes

5% Alcohols

1% Esters

12% Other

Note

- True melissa oil is rare and costly so is often adulterated with either lemon or lemongrass. Be sure to purchase from a reputable dealer.

- Melissa is also known as lemon balm and has a lemony scent.

- Research in Germany has found melissa to possess antiviral properties against viruses linked to influenza, herpes and mumps.

- Research on melissa's sedative properties found that sedation increased slightly between thirty and sixty minutes after application and remained for two hours. Only small amounts of the oil were needed.

Caution

- Avoid during pregnancy.

- May cause irritation or sensitisation in some people so use well diluted.

Melissa

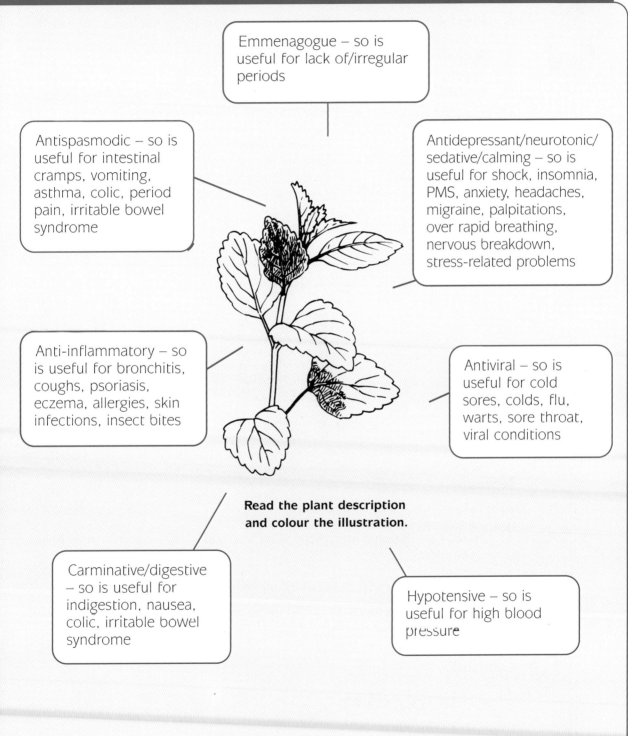

Emmenagogue – so is useful for lack of/irregular periods

Antispasmodic – so is useful for intestinal cramps, vomiting, asthma, colic, period pain, irritable bowel syndrome

Antidepressant/neurotonic/ sedative/calming – so is useful for shock, insomnia, PMS, anxiety, headaches, migraine, palpitations, over rapid breathing, nervous breakdown, stress-related problems

Anti-inflammatory – so is useful for bronchitis, coughs, psoriasis, eczema, allergies, skin infections, insect bites

Antiviral – so is useful for cold sores, colds, flu, warts, sore throat, viral conditions

Read the plant description and colour the illustration.

Carminative/digestive – so is useful for indigestion, nausea, colic, irritable bowel syndrome

Hypotensive – so is useful for high blood pressure

COMMIPHORA MYRRHA – MYRRH

- **Plant description:** Small tree with aromatic green leaves and small white flowers
- **Botanical family:** Burseraceae
- **Note:** Base
- **Extraction:** Incisions are made into the bark of the tree and yellow-coloured resin exudes out from it. It hardens and becomes a reddish-brown colour, known as myrrh. The myrrh is steam distilled to produce the oil.
- **Production:** Originated in parts of Africa and Asia. Grown in semi-desert regions such as Libya, Iran and near the Red Sea.
- **Blends well with:** Frankincense, lavender, patchouli, rose, rosewood, sandalwood, tea tree, thyme

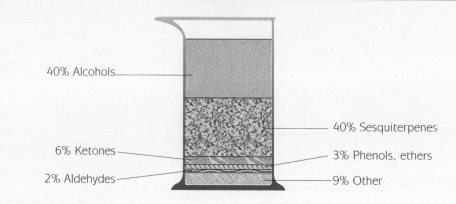

40% Alcohols

40% Sesquiterpenes

6% Ketones

3% Phenols, ethers

2% Aldehydes

9% Other

Notes

- There are several species of myrrh.
- Myrrh is a traditional ingredient of incense and is often used for religious ceremonies.
- Myrrh was often used in Egypt for embalming.
- Frankincense and myrrh are from the same botanical family so share many properties.

Caution

- Avoid during pregnancy.

Myrrh

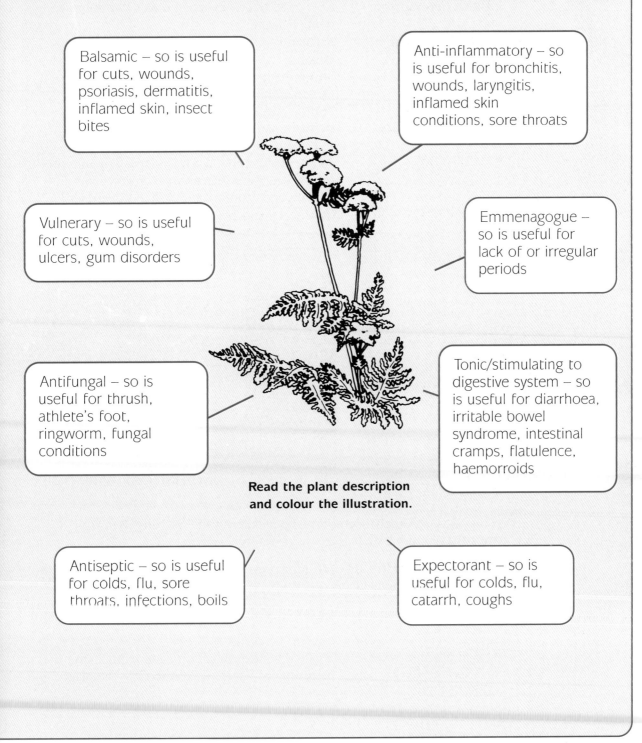

Balsamic – so is useful for cuts, wounds, psoriasis, dermatitis, inflamed skin, insect bites

Anti-inflammatory – so is useful for bronchitis, wounds, laryngitis, inflamed skin conditions, sore throats

Vulnerary – so is useful for cuts, wounds, ulcers, gum disorders

Emmenagogue – so is useful for lack of or irregular periods

Antifungal – so is useful for thrush, athlete's foot, ringworm, fungal conditions

Tonic/stimulating to digestive system – so is useful for diarrhoea, irritable bowel syndrome, intestinal cramps, flatulence, haemorroids

Read the plant description and colour the illustration.

Antiseptic – so is useful for colds, flu, sore throats, infections, boils

Expectorant – so is useful for colds, flu, catarrh, coughs

CITRUS AURANTIUM VAR. AMARA – NEROLI (ORANGE BLOSSOM)

- **Plant description:** Evergreen tree with green leaves and fragrant white flowers
- **Botanical family:** Rutaceae
- **Note:** Base
- **Extraction:** Steam distillation or enfleurage of the flowers
- **Production:** Originated in China. Produced in Morocco, Tunisia and France.
- **Blends well with:** Benzoin, bergamot, cedarwood, chamomile (German and Roman), clary sage, frankincense, geranium, jasmine, lavender, lemon, mandarin, myrrh, orange, rose, rosemary, rosewood, sandalwood, ylang-ylang. It blends well with most floral and citrus oils.

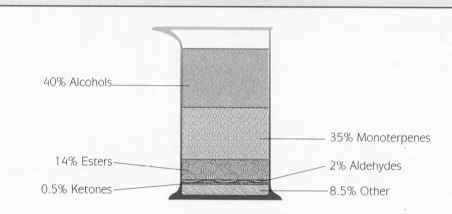

40% Alcohols
35% Monoterpenes
14% Esters
2% Aldehydes
0.5% Ketones
8.5% Other

Notes

- A concrete and absolute is also produced by solvent extraction of the freshly picked flowers.

- This oil is extremely useful for anxiety states and especially useful for stressful situations such as exams or interviews.

- Neroli and mandarin are useful for preventing stretch marks when rubbed into the skin.

- The distillation water, orange flower water, is often used as a toner or to add to clay masks.

- Neroli was discovered in the late seventeenth century and named after the princess of Nerola, Italy. The people of Venice used it to fight the plague and other fevers.

Neroli (orange blossom)

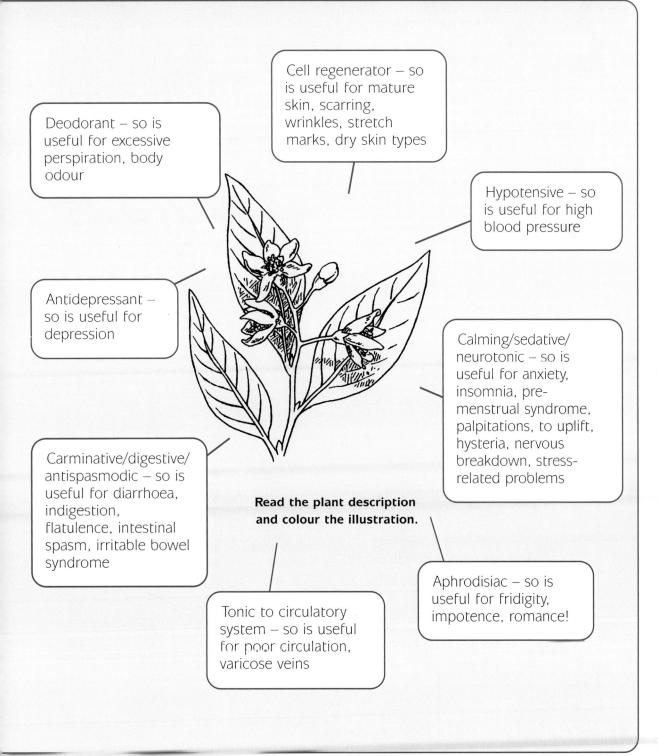

Cell regenerator – so is useful for mature skin, scarring, wrinkles, stretch marks, dry skin types

Deodorant – so is useful for excessive perspiration, body odour

Hypotensive – so is useful for high blood pressure

Antidepressant – so is useful for depression

Calming/sedative/ neurotonic – so is useful for anxiety, insomnia, pre- menstrual syndrome, palpitations, to uplift, hysteria, nervous breakdown, stress- related problems

Carminative/digestive/ antispasmodic – so is useful for diarrhoea, indigestion, flatulence, intestinal spasm, irritable bowel syndrome

Read the plant description and colour the illustration.

Aphrodisiac – so is useful for fridigity, impotence, romance!

Tonic to circulatory system – so is useful for poor circulation, varicose veins

CITRUS SINENSIS – ORANGE (SWEET)

- **Plant description:** Evergreen tree with green, spear-shaped leaves bearing orange fruit
- **Botanical family:** Rutaceae
- **Note:** Top
- **Extraction:** Expressed from the peel of the fruit, sometimes steam distilled
- **Production:** Originated in China. Now grown in the Mediterranean, California, Israel and South America.
- **Blends well with:** Bergamot, clary sage, clove, cypress, frankincense, geranium, grapefruit, jasmine, juniper, lavender, myrrh, neroli, petitgrain, rose, rosewood, sandalwood, ylang-ylang

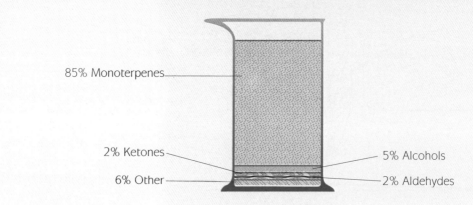

85% Monoterpenes

2% Ketones

6% Other

5% Alcohols

2% Aldehydes

Notes

- The properties of the orange (citrus oil) overlap with many properties associated with neroli (flower oil).

- Orange that has been extracted by expression is of a higher quality than oil that has been steam distilled.

- Using orange oil helps to bring joy and positive energy to the body.

Orange (sweet)

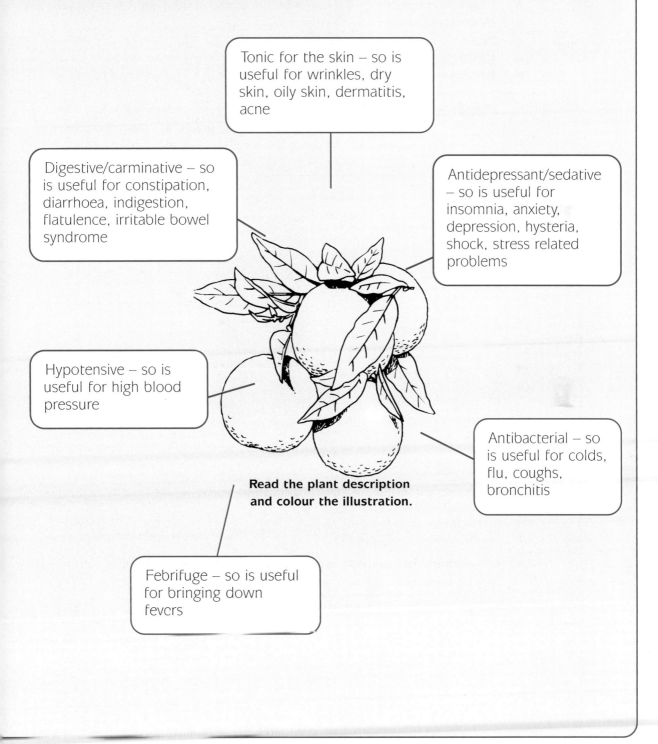

Tonic for the skin – so is useful for wrinkles, dry skin, oily skin, dermatitis, acne

Digestive/carminative – so is useful for constipation, diarrhoea, indigestion, flatulence, irritable bowel syndrome

Antidepressant/sedative – so is useful for insomnia, anxiety, depression, hysteria, shock, stress related problems

Hypotensive – so is useful for high blood pressure

Antibacterial – so is useful for colds, flu, coughs, bronchitis

Read the plant description and colour the illustration.

Febrifuge – so is useful for bringing down fevers

POGOSTEMON CABLIN – PATCHOULI

- **Plant description:** Herb with large green leaves and white flowers
- **Botanical family:** Lamiaceae
- **Note:** Base
- **Extraction:** Steam distillation of the leaves
- **Production:** Originated in tropical Asia. Produced in India, Malaysia and Indonesia.

- **Blends well with:** Bergamot, black pepper, cedarwood, clary sage, clove, frankincense, geranium, ginger, lavender, lemongrass, myrrh, neroli, rose, rosewood, sandalwood, valerian, vetiver, ylang-ylang

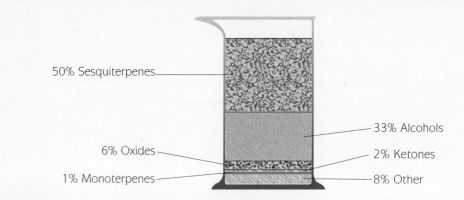

50% Sesquiterpenes
33% Alcohols
6% Oxides
2% Ketones
1% Monoterpenes
8% Other

Notes

- Often used as a fixative in perfumes as it helps to prolong the aroma.

- Many people dislike the smell of patchouli, so ensure the client has smelt the blend prior to using.

- The name 'patchouli' originated from India where it was used as an antidote against insect and snake bites.

- The essential oil is thick and dark brown, often with a green tinge.

- The chemical patchoulene found in patchouli is very similar in structure to azulene (found in chamomile) and has the same anti-inflammatory properties.

Pogostemon cablin

Patchouli

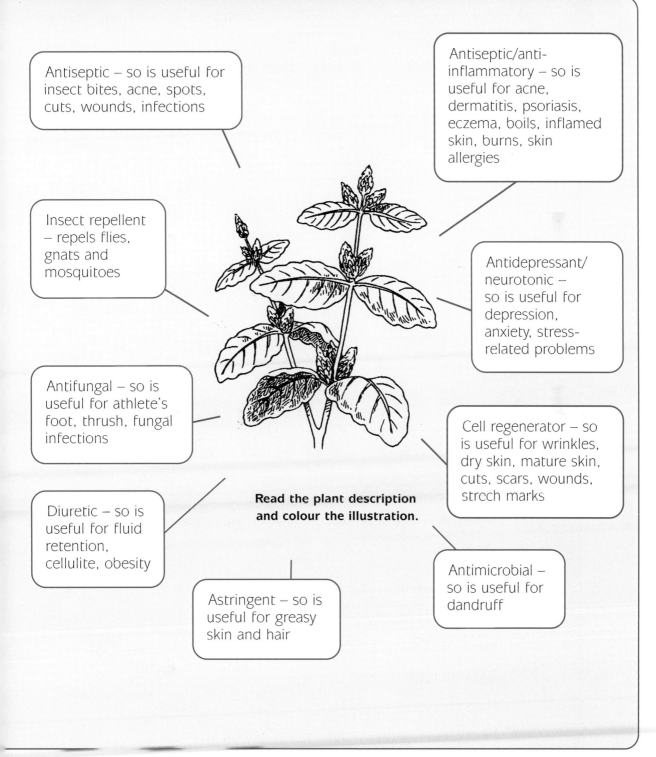

Antiseptic – so is useful for insect bites, acne, spots, cuts, wounds, infections

Antiseptic/anti-inflammatory – so is useful for acne, dermatitis, psoriasis, eczema, boils, inflamed skin, burns, skin allergies

Insect repellent – repels flies, gnats and mosquitoes

Antidepressant/neurotonic – so is useful for depression, anxiety, stress-related problems

Antifungal – so is useful for athlete's foot, thrush, fungal infections

Cell regenerator – so is useful for wrinkles, dry skin, mature skin, cuts, scars, wounds, strech marks

Diuretic – so is useful for fluid retention, cellulite, obesity

Read the plant description and colour the illustration.

Astringent – so is useful for greasy skin and hair

Antimicrobial – so is useful for dandruff

MENTHA PIPERITA – PEPPERMINT

- **Plant description:** Herb with small green leaves and pink-mauve flowers
- **Botanical family:** Lamiaceae
- **Note:** Middle
- **Extraction:** Steam distillation of the leaves and flowering tops
- **Production:** Originated in Europe but now is mostly produced in the USA.
- **Blends well with:** Basil, benzoin, bergamot, cajeput, cedarwood, cypress, eucalyptus, fennel, lemon, mandarin, marjoram, pine, rosemary, thyme

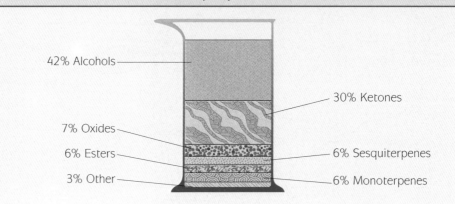

42% Alcohols
30% Ketones
7% Oxides
6% Esters
3% Other
6% Sesquiterpenes
6% Monoterpenes

Notes

- Peppermint tea can be recommended and is helpful for digestive complaints.
- English plants are said to produce the best oil because of the climate.
- This is used to flavour toothpaste and confectionery and in medicine.
- Peppermint can be used to repel nuisance insects or animals and will not harm children or animals.
- Peppermint is used in the medicine Colpermin, to treat irritable bowel syndrome.

Caution

- Do not use in conjunction with homeopathic remedies.
- May cause sensitisation in some people.
- May irritate during high doses.
- Avoid during pregnancy.
- Do not use on young children.
- Do not use peppermint before bedtime as it is a stimulant.

Peppermint

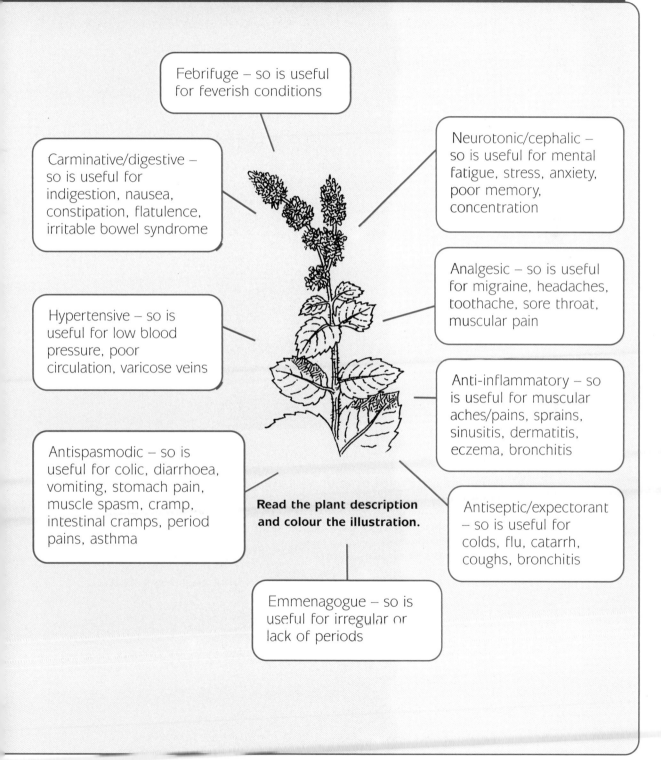

Febrifuge – so is useful for feverish conditions

Neurotonic/cephalic – so is useful for mental fatigue, stress, anxiety, poor memory, concentration

Carminative/digestive – so is useful for indigestion, nausea, constipation, flatulence, irritable bowel syndrome

Analgesic – so is useful for migraine, headaches, toothache, sore throat, muscular pain

Hypertensive – so is useful for low blood pressure, poor circulation, varicose veins

Anti-inflammatory – so is useful for muscular aches/pains, sprains, sinusitis, dermatitis, eczema, bronchitis

Antispasmodic – so is useful for colic, diarrhoea, vomiting, stomach pain, muscle spasm, cramp, intestinal cramps, period pains, asthma

Read the plant description and colour the illustration.

Antiseptic/expectorant – so is useful for colds, flu, catarrh, coughs, bronchitis

Emmenagogue – so is useful for irregular or lack of periods

CITRUS AURANTIUM VAR. AMARA – PETITGRAIN

- **Plant description:** Evergreen tree with green leaves and fragrant white flowers
- **Botanical family:** Rutaceae
- **Note:** Top
- **Extraction:** Steam distillation of the leaves and twigs of the bitter orange tree
- **Production:** Originated in China. The best quality petitgrain comes from France and North Africa.
- **Blends well with:** Benzoin, bergamot, cedarwood, clary sage, clove, geranium, lavender, lemongrass, jasmine, neroli, orange, rosemary, rosewood, sandalwood, valerian, ylang-ylang

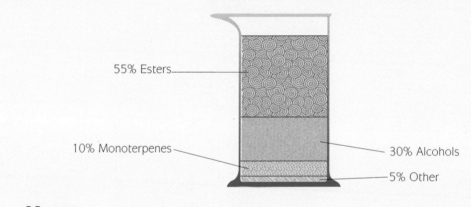

55% Esters

10% Monoterpenes

30% Alcohols

5% Other

Notes

- Petitgrain is extracted from the same tree as neroli and orange oils.

- In earlier centuries petitgrain used to be extracted from the unripe oranges, which were small and green, hence 'petit grains', which means little grains.

- Petitgrain is not phototoxic so can be used instead of bergamot if necessary.

- Petitgrain has similar properties to neroli, although is less sedative.

Petitgrain

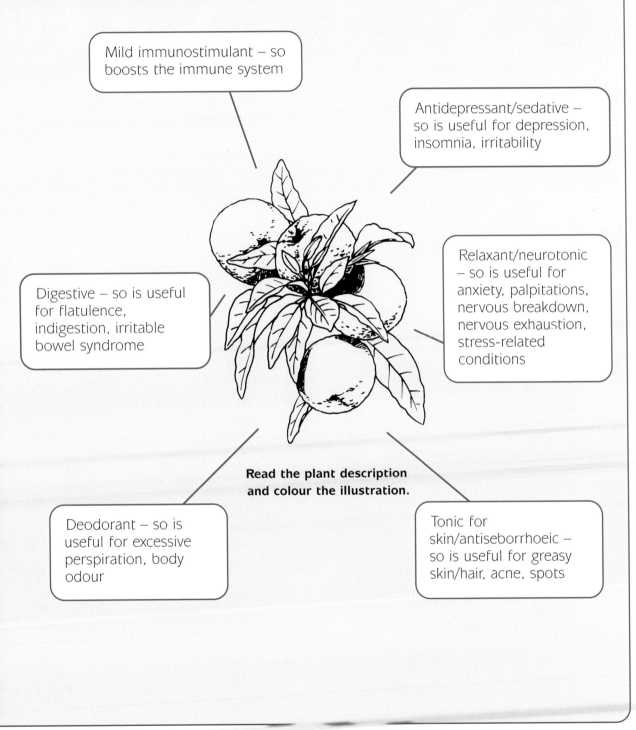

Mild immunostimulant – so boosts the immune system

Antidepressant/sedative – so is useful for depression, insomnia, irritability

Relaxant/neurotonic – so is useful for anxiety, palpitations, nervous breakdown, nervous exhaustion, stress-related conditions

Digestive – so is useful for flatulence, indigestion, irritable bowel syndrome

Read the plant description and colour the illustration.

Deodorant – so is useful for excessive perspiration, body odour

Tonic for skin/antiseborrhoeic – so is useful for greasy skin/hair, acne, spots

PINUS SYLVESTRIS – PINE (SCOTCH)

- **Plant description:** Tall evergreen tree with reddish bark, green spiky needles and brown cones
- **Botanical family:** Pinaceae
- **Note:** Middle
- **Extraction:** Steam distillation of the pine needles, sometimes twigs and cones
- **Production:** Originated in Northern Europe and North America. Produced in France, Canada and Russia.
- **Blends well with:** Bergamot, cajeput, cedarwood, clove, cypress, eucalyptus, lavender, marjoram, peppermint, rosemary, tea tree, thyme, valerian

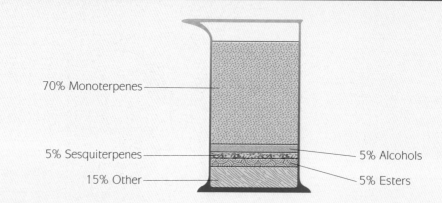

70% Monoterpenes
5% Sesquiterpenes
15% Other
5% Alcohols
5% Esters

Notes

- Pine oil is obtained from many species of pine: ensure you are familiar with the botanical name as dwarf pine (*Pinus pumilio*) is classed as a hazardous oil.

- Pine is added to many commercial products because of its fresh smell, especially bath products and cleaning agents.

- Many varieties of pine, such as longleaf pine, are used to produce turpentine, found in paint remover!

- Native Americans used to stuff mattresses with pine needles to repel lice and fleas.

Caution

- May cause irritation or sensitisation to the skin.

Pine (Scotch)

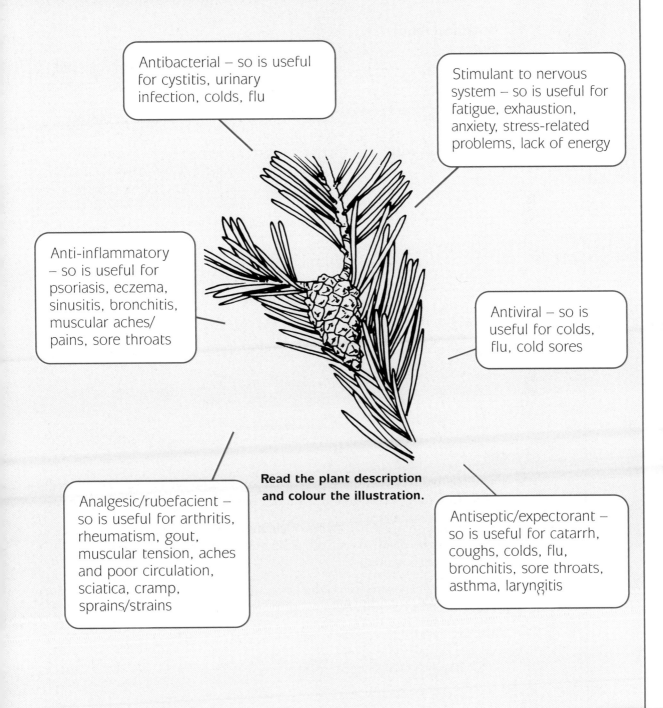

Antibacterial – so is useful for cystitis, urinary infection, colds, flu

Stimulant to nervous system – so is useful for fatigue, exhaustion, anxiety, stress-related problems, lack of energy

Anti-inflammatory – so is useful for psoriasis, eczema, sinusitis, bronchitis, muscular aches/pains, sore throats

Antiviral – so is useful for colds, flu, cold sores

Read the plant description and colour the illustration.

Analgesic/rubefacient – so is useful for arthritis, rheumatism, gout, muscular tension, aches and poor circulation, sciatica, cramp, sprains/strains

Antiseptic/expectorant – so is useful for catarrh, coughs, colds, flu, bronchitis, sore throats, asthma, laryngitis

ROSA CENTIFOLIA – ROSE (CABBAGE)

- **Plant description:** A shrub with green leaves and large pink or rosy purple petals.
- **Botanical family:** Rosaceae
- **Note:** Middle
- **Extraction:** Steam distilled from the petals. A concrete and absolute are produced by solvent extraction from the fresh petals.
- **Production:** Originated in Morocco. Produced in Morocco, Italy and France.
- **Blends well with:** Bergamot, carrot, chamomile (German and Roman), clary sage, fennel, frankincense, geranium, jasmine, lavender, melissa, myrrh, neroli, patchouli, rosewood, sandalwood, ylang-ylang and most other oils

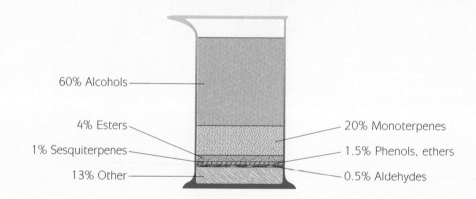

60% Alcohols
4% Esters
1% Sesquiterpenes
13% Other
20% Monoterpenes
1.5% Phenols, ethers
0.5% Aldehydes

Notes

- There are two types of rose – *Rosa damascena* and *Rosa centifolia*. The oils are slightly different in colour and fragrance but have very similar properties.

- Rose absolute may contain traces of chemical solvents that can be toxic. It is better to choose distilled rose oil, or an absolute that has been extracted by the carbon dioxide method.

- Rose is a very expensive oil as the petals of thirty roses are needed to produce just one drop of rose oil.

- There are over 10,000 types of cultivated rose.

Rose (cabbage)

Haemostatic – so is useful for wounds, cuts, nosebleeds

Emmenagogue – so is useful for irregular or lack of periods

Antidepressant/ neurotonic/sedative – so is useful for depression, headaches, anxiety, pre-menstrual syndrome, insomnia, stress related problems, postnatal depression

Astringent – so is useful for dilated capillaries, mature skin, wrinkles, poor circulation

Aphrodisiac – so is useful for fridigity, impotence, romance!

Anti-inflammatory – so is useful for bronchitis, conjunctivitis, eczema, coughs, inflamed skin, hay fever

Read the plant description and colour the illustration.

Antiviral/antiseptic – so is useful for infections, wounds, coughs, sore throat, cold sores

Cell regenerator/rehydrating – so is useful for dehydrated, dry, mature skin, cracked skin, dermatitis, psoriasis, eczema

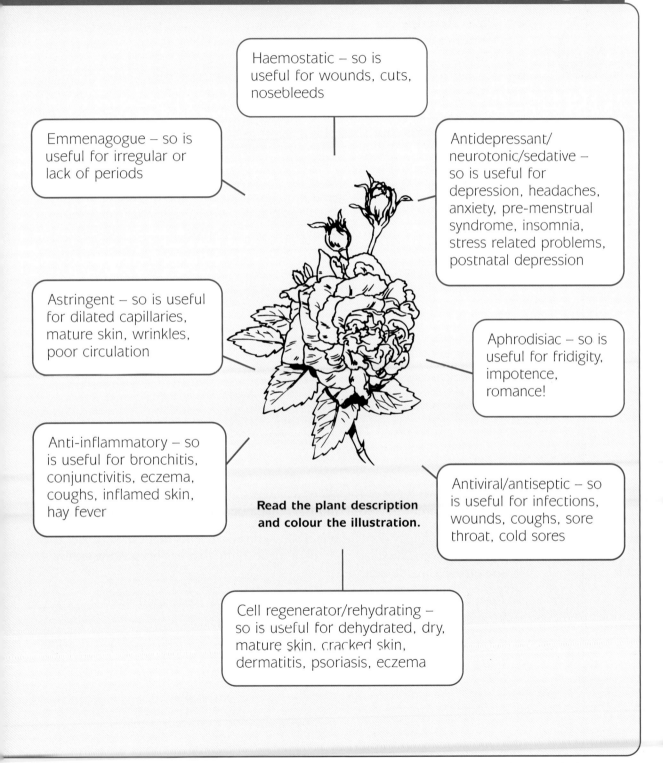

ROSA DAMASCENA – ROSE DAMASK (ALSO KNOWN AS ROSE OTTO)

- **Plant description:** Shrub with green leaves and pink flowers
- **Botanical family:** Rosaceae
- **Note:** Middle
- **Extraction:** Steam distilled from the petals. A concrete and absolute are produced by solvent extraction from the fresh petals.
- **Production:** Originated in Morocco. Produced in Bulgaria, Turkey and France.
- **Blends well with:** Bergamot, carrot, chamomile (German and Roman), clary sage, fennel, frankincense, geranium, jasmine, lavender, melissa, myrrh, neroli, patchouli, rosewood, sandalwood, ylang-ylang and most other oils.

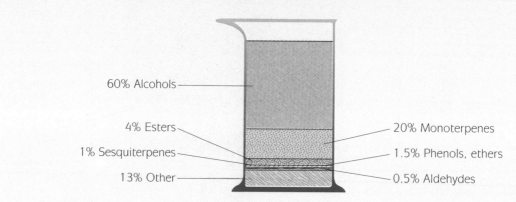

60% Alcohols

4% Esters

1% Sesquiterpenes

13% Other

20% Monoterpenes

1.5% Phenols, ethers

0.5% Aldehydes

Notes

There are two types of rose: *Rosa damascena* and *Rosa centifolia*. The oils are slightly different in colour and fragrance but have very similar properties.

Rose absolute may contain traces of chemical solvents that can be toxic. It is better to choose distilled rose oil or an absolute that has been extracted by the carbon dioxide method.

Rose is a very expensive oil as the petals of thirty roses are needed to produce one drop of rose oil.

A by-product of rose oil distillation is rose water, which is used as a facial toner or can be added to mask ingredients.

Rose (damask)
also known as rose otto

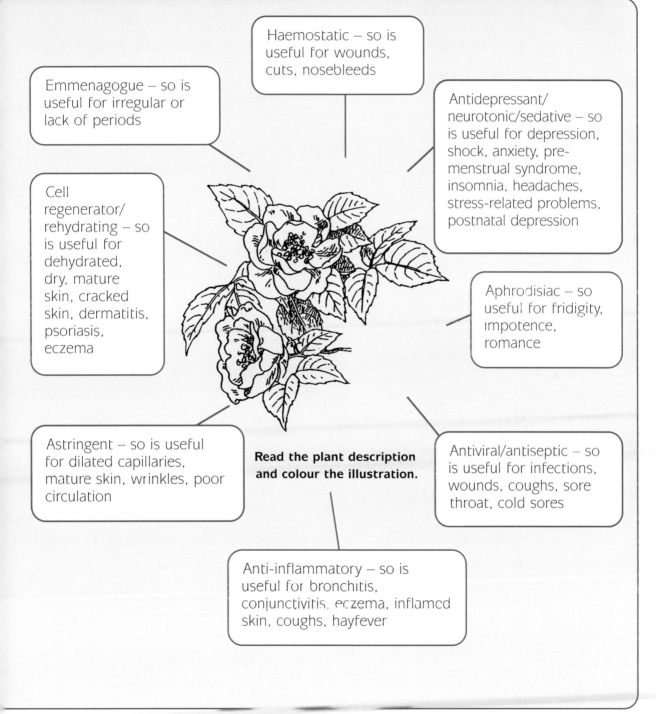

Haemostatic – so is useful for wounds, cuts, nosebleeds

Emmenagogue – so is useful for irregular or lack of periods

Antidepressant/ neurotonic/sedative – so is useful for depression, shock, anxiety, pre- menstrual syndrome, insomnia, headaches, stress-related problems, postnatal depression

Cell regenerator/ rehydrating – so is useful for dehydrated, dry, mature skin, cracked skin, dermatitis, psoriasis, eczema

Aphrodisiac – so useful for fridigity, impotence, romance

Astringent – so is useful for dilated capillaries, mature skin, wrinkles, poor circulation

Read the plant description and colour the illustration.

Antiviral/antiseptic – so is useful for infections, wounds, coughs, sore throat, cold sores

Anti-inflammatory – so is useful for bronchitis, conjunctivitis, eczema, inflamed skin, coughs, hayfever

ESSENTIAL OIL NOTES

ROSMARINUS OFFICINALIS – ROSEMARY

- **Plant description:** Herb with spiky green leaves and tiny blue flowers
- **Botanical family:** Lamiaceae
- **Note:** Middle
- **Extraction:** Steam distillation of the flowering tops and from the stems and leaves
- **Production:** Originated in the Mediterranean area. Produced in Tunisia, Algeria, France and Hungary.
- **Blends well with:** Basil, bergamot, black pepper, cajeput, carrot, cedarwood, fennel, frankincense, geranium, ginger, grapefuit, lavender, lemon, lemongrass, mandarin, marjoram, orange, peppermint, petitgrain, pine, tea tree, thyme

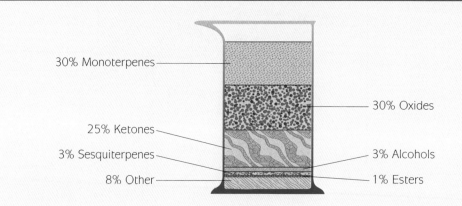

30% Monoterpenes — 30% Oxides
25% Ketones — 3% Alcohols
3% Sesquiterpenes — 1% Esters
8% Other

Notes

- Rosemary is an excellent brain stimulant and can be used prior to interviews or examination.

- Rosemary is a good tonic for the heart and liver, and is thought to help lower cholesterol levels in the blood.

- It is said that rosemary can restore colour to grey hair and even cure baldness!

- Rosemary was burnt in hospital wards in France up until the early 1900s, due to its powerful antiseptic properties.

Caution

- Do not use on people with epilepsy or high blood pressure.

- Avoid during pregnancy.

Aromatherapy for Holistic Therapists

Rosemary

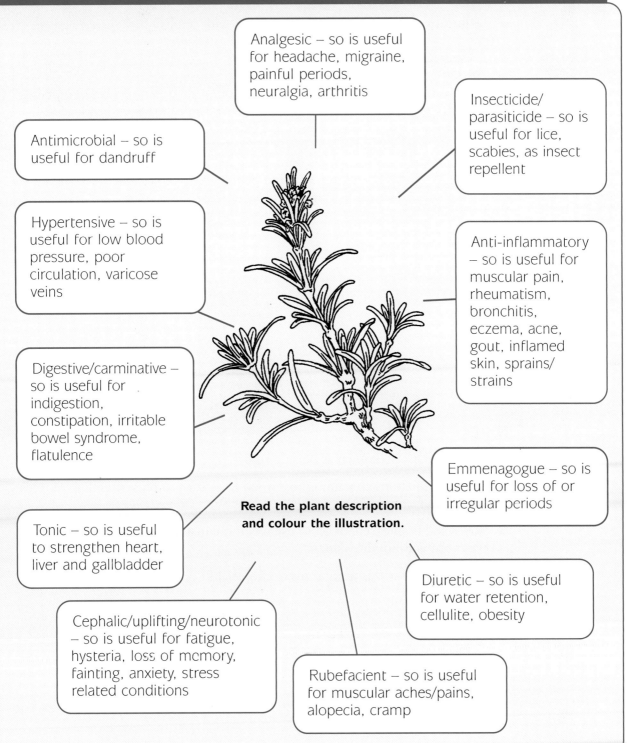

Analgesic – so is useful for headache, migraine, painful periods, neuralgia, arthritis

Insecticide/parasiticide – so is useful for lice, scabies, as insect repellent

Antimicrobial – so is useful for dandruff

Hypertensive – so is useful for low blood pressure, poor circulation, varicose veins

Anti-inflammatory – so is useful for muscular pain, rheumatism, bronchitis, eczema, acne, gout, inflamed skin, sprains/strains

Digestive/carminative – so is useful for indigestion, constipation, irritable bowel syndrome, flatulence

Emmenagogue – so is useful for loss of or irregular periods

Read the plant description and colour the illustration.

Tonic – so is useful to strengthen heart, liver and gallbladder

Diuretic – so is useful for water retention, cellulite, obesity

Cephalic/uplifting/neurotonic – so is useful for fatigue, hysteria, loss of memory, fainting, anxiety, stress related conditions

Rubefacient – so is useful for muscular aches/pains, alopecia, cramp

ANIBA ROSAEODORA – ROSEWOOD

- **Plant description:** Evergreen tree with reddish bark, green leaves and bearing yellow flowers
- **Botanical family:** Lauraceae
- **Note:** Middle
- **Extraction:** Steam distillation of the rosewood bark chippings
- **Production:** Originated in the Amazon region. Produced in Brazil and Peru.
- **Blends well with:** Bergamot, cedarwood, frankincense, geranium, jasmine, lavender, mandarin, neroli, orange, patchouli, petitgrain, rose, rosemary, sandalwood, vetiver, ylang-ylang

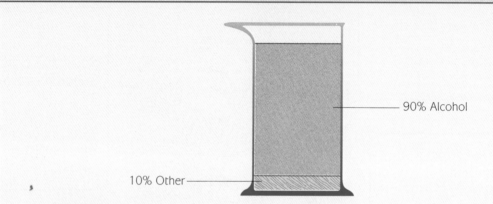

90% Alcohol

10% Other

Notes

- Rosewood is also known as bois de rose.

- Special plantations containing rosewood trees exist to prevent felling of trees in the Amazon rainforest.

- Rosewood is an excellent oil to use when meditating as it gives a calming effect but without drowsiness.

- In Japan rosewood is used to make chopsticks.

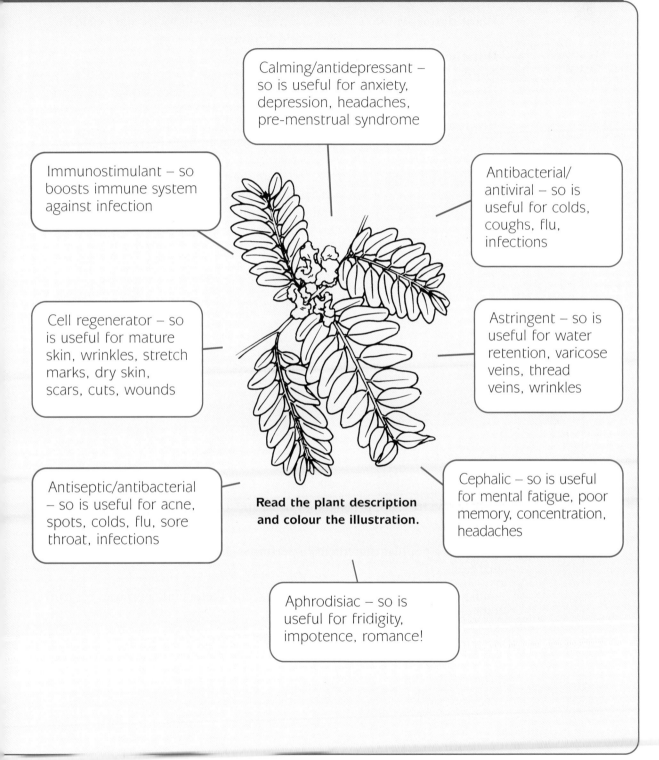

Calming/antidepressant – so is useful for anxiety, depression, headaches, pre-menstrual syndrome

Immunostimulant – so boosts immune system against infection

Antibacterial/antiviral – so is useful for colds, coughs, flu, infections

Cell regenerator – so is useful for mature skin, wrinkles, stretch marks, dry skin, scars, cuts, wounds

Astringent – so is useful for water retention, varicose veins, thread veins, wrinkles

Antiseptic/antibacterial – so is useful for acne, spots, colds, flu, sore throat, infections

Cephalic – so is useful for mental fatigue, poor memory, concentration, headaches

Read the plant description and colour the illustration.

Aphrodisiac – so is useful for fridigity, impotence, romance!

SANTALUM ALBUM – SANDALWOOD

- **Plant description:** Evergreen tree with green leaves and small, pinky/purple flowers
- **Botanical family:** Santalaceae
- **Note:** Base
- **Extraction:** Steam distillation of the heartwood at the centre of the tree
- **Production:** Originated in tropical Asia. Produced in Asia. The region of Mysore in India exports the highest quality oil.
- **Blends well with:** Basil, benzoin, bergamot, black pepper, carrot, cedarwood, clove, cypress, fennel, frankincense, geranium, jasmine, lavender, lemon, myrrh, neroli, orange, patchouli, rose, vetiver, ylang-ylang

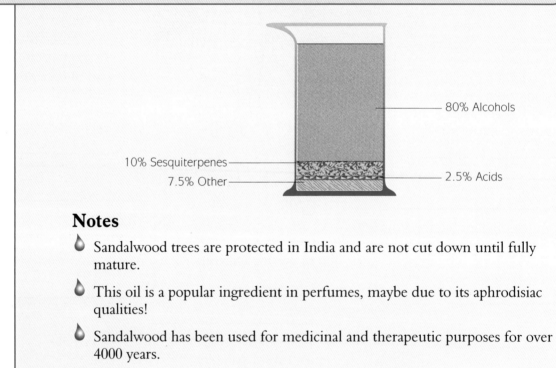

80% Alcohols

10% Sesquiterpenes

7.5% Other

2.5% Acids

Notes

- Sandalwood trees are protected in India and are not cut down until fully mature.

- This oil is a popular ingredient in perfumes, maybe due to its aphrodisiac qualities!

- Sandalwood has been used for medicinal and therapeutic purposes for over 4000 years.

Sandalwood

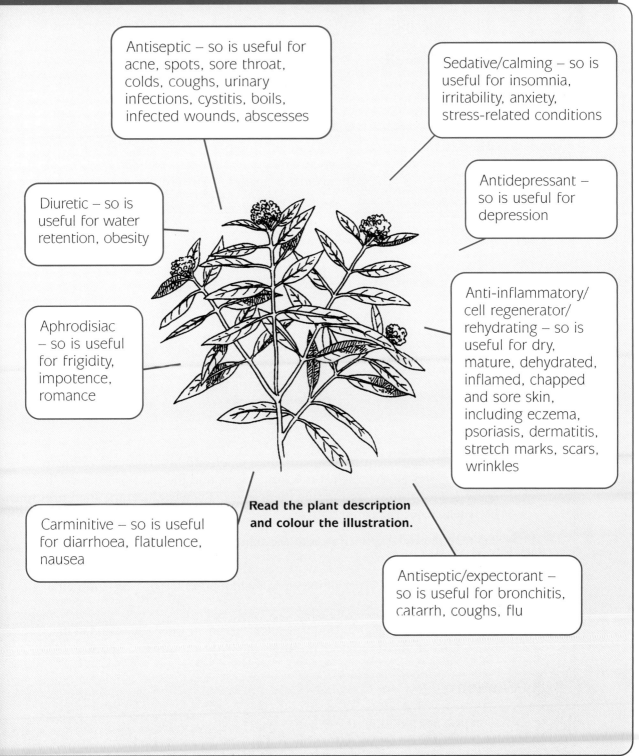

Antiseptic – so is useful for acne, spots, sore throat, colds, coughs, urinary infections, cystitis, boils, infected wounds, abscesses

Sedative/calming – so is useful for insomnia, irritability, anxiety, stress-related conditions

Antidepressant – so is useful for depression

Diuretic – so is useful for water retention, obesity

Aphrodisiac – so is useful for frigidity, impotence, romance

Anti-inflammatory/cell regenerator/rehydrating – so is useful for dry, mature, dehydrated, inflamed, chapped and sore skin, including eczema, psoriasis, dermatitis, stretch marks, scars, wrinkles

Read the plant description and colour the illustration.

Carminitive – so is useful for diarrhoea, flatulence, nausea

Antiseptic/expectorant – so is useful for bronchitis, catarrh, coughs, flu

MELALEUCA ALTERNIFOLIA – TEA TREE (SOMETIMES CALLED TI TREE)

- **Plant description:** A small tree with needle-like green leaves and yellow or purplish flowers
- **Botanical family:** Myrtaceae
- **Note:** Top
- **Extraction:** Steam distillation of the leaves and twigs
- **Production:** Tea tree orginates and is grown in New South Wales in Australia
- **Blends well with:** Cajeput, chamomile, clove, cypress, eucalyptus, geranium, ginger, juniper, lavender, lemon, mandarin, marjoram, myrrh, orange, peppermint, pine, rosemary, thyme

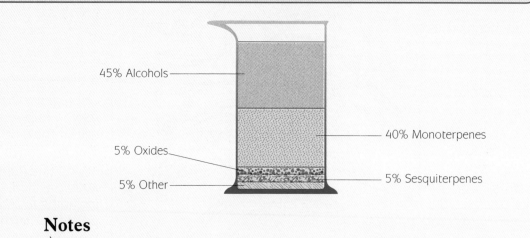

45% Alcohols
40% Monoterpenes
5% Oxides
5% Other
5% Sesquiterpenes

Notes

- In the eighteenth century Captain James Cook and his crew, on landing in Australia, noticed that the tea tree growing around the lakes had turned the water reddish-brown, reminding them of tea. They began to use the leaves to brew tea, hence the name tea tree.

- Tea tree oil can be applied neat to the skin and is useful for cold sores, verrucae and warts.

- Tea tree combats all types of infection including bacterial, fungal and viral infections.

- This oil is an effective immunostimulant, so when the body is under attack by bacteria or viruses tea tree increases the body's ability to respond.

Caution

- Possible sensitisation in some people.

Tea tree
(sometimes called Ti tree)

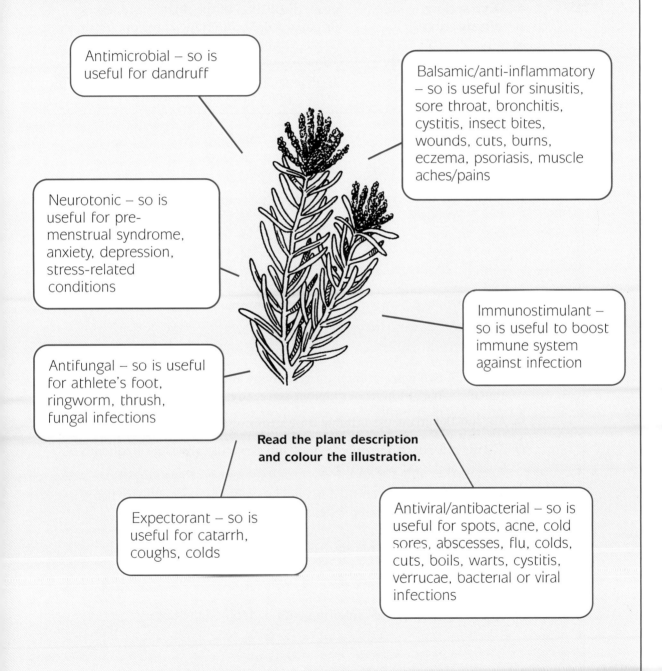

Antimicrobial – so is useful for dandruff

Balsamic/anti-inflammatory – so is useful for sinusitis, sore throat, bronchitis, cystitis, insect bites, wounds, cuts, burns, eczema, psoriasis, muscle aches/pains

Neurotonic – so is useful for pre-menstrual syndrome, anxiety, depression, stress-related conditions

Immunostimulant – so is useful to boost immune system against infection

Antifungal – so is useful for athlete's foot, ringworm, thrush, fungal infections

Read the plant description and colour the illustration.

Expectorant – so is useful for catarrh, coughs, colds

Antiviral/antibacterial – so is useful for spots, acne, cold sores, abscesses, flu, colds, cuts, boils, warts, cystitis, verrucae, bacterial or viral infections

ESSENTIAL OIL NOTES

THYMUS VULGARIS – THYME (RED)

- **Plant description:** Herb with tiny green leaves and pink-lilac flowers
- **Botanical family:** Lamiaceae
- **Note:** Top
- **Extraction:** Steam distillation of the flowers and leaves
- **Production:** Originated in Mediterranean region. Produced in Russia, China and the USA.
- **Blends well with:** Bergamot, cajeput, cedarwood, chamomile, eucalyptus, juniper, lavender, lemon, mandarin, melissa, pine, rosemary, tea tree

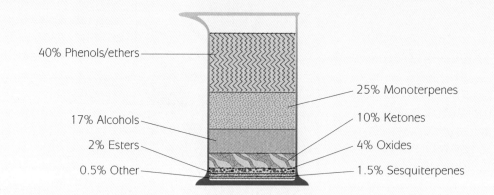

40% Phenols/ethers
17% Alcohols
2% Esters
0.5% Other
25% Monoterpenes
10% Ketones
4% Oxides
1.5% Sesquiterpenes

Notes

- There are two types of thyme – red thyme and sweet thyme. Red thyme contains large amounts of phenols; sweet thyme contains mostly alcohols.
- Ancient Egyptians used thyme for embalming their dead.
- Thyme oils contain mainly thymol and carvacol, which are frequently isolated and used in pharmacy.
- Thyme has always been used in cooking and like most culinary herbs is beneficial to the digestive system.

Caution

- Avoid during pregnancy.
- Do not use on people suffering with high blood pressure.

Thyme (red)

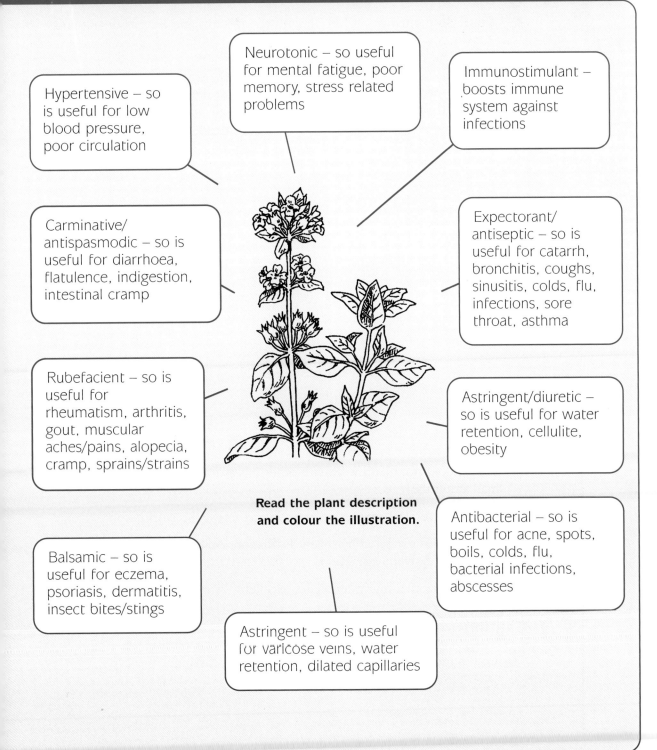

Neurotonic – so useful for mental fatigue, poor memory, stress related problems

Immunostimulant – boosts immune system against infections

Hypertensive – so is useful for low blood pressure, poor circulation

Carminative/ antispasmodic – so is useful for diarrhoea, flatulence, indigestion, intestinal cramp

Expectorant/ antiseptic – so is useful for catarrh, bronchitis, coughs, sinusitis, colds, flu, infections, sore throat, asthma

Rubefacient – so is useful for rheumatism, arthritis, gout, muscular aches/pains, alopecia, cramp, sprains/strains

Astringent/diuretic – so is useful for water retention, cellulite, obesity

Read the plant description and colour the illustration.

Antibacterial – so is useful for acne, spots, boils, colds, flu, bacterial infections, abscesses

Balsamic – so is useful for eczema, psoriasis, dermatitis, insect bites/stings

Astringent – so is useful for varicose veins, water retention, dilated capillaries

VALERIANA FAURIEI – VALERIAN

- **Plant description:** Herb with green stems and leaves bearing pink and white flowers
- **Botanical family:** Valerianaceae
- **Note:** Base
- **Extraction:** Steam distillation of the rhizomes
- **Production:** Originated in Europe and parts of Asia. Produced in Belgium, France, UK, China and Russia.
- **Blends well with:** Lavender, mandarin, patchouli, petitgrain, pine, rosemary

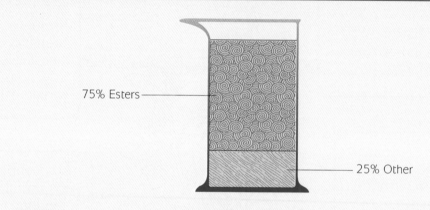

75% Esters

25% Other

Notes

- This oil does not blend well with other oils as it has a strong smell. Only use small amounts.

- There are over 150 types of valerian found across the world.

- Essential oil is extracted by steam distillation. An absolute and concrete are extracted by solvent extraction.

- Herbal teas containing valerian are excellent for relaxing and calming.

Caution

Use in moderation to prevent sensitisation occurring.

Valerian

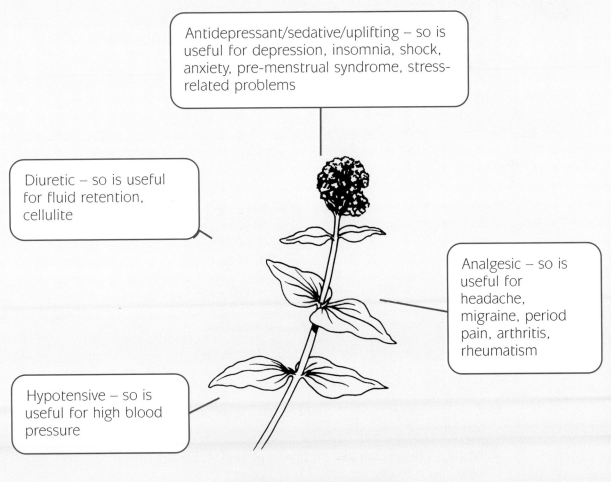

Antidepressant/sedative/uplifting – so is useful for depression, insomnia, shock, anxiety, pre-menstrual syndrome, stress-related problems

Diuretic – so is useful for fluid retention, cellulite

Analgesic – so is useful for headache, migraine, period pain, arthritis, rheumatism

Hypotensive – so is useful for high blood pressure

Read the plant description and colour the illustration.

VETIVERIA ZIZANOIDES – VETIVER

- **Plant description:** Tall, scented green grass with long narrow leaves
- **Botanical family:** Gramineae
- **Note:** Base
- **Extraction:** Steam distillation of the roots
- **Production:** Originally in India, Indonesia and Sri Lanka. Produced in Java, Haiti, Europe and the USA.
- **Blends well with:** Bergamot, clary sage, frankincense, geranium, grapefruit, jasmine, lavender, lemon, lemongrass, mandarin, orange, patchouli, rose, sandalwood, ylang-ylang

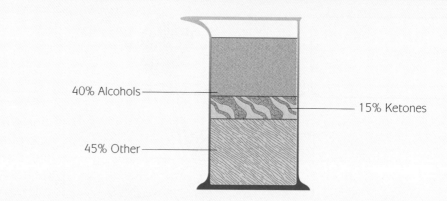

40% Alcohols

15% Ketones

45% Other

Notes

Vetiver oil is dark brown and thick in consistency.

If used sparingly vetiver could be used as an alternative base note in virtually any blend.

Many people do not like the aroma of vetiver. Ensure the client smells the blend prior to use.

In India and Sri Lanka vetiver is known as the oil of tranquillity.

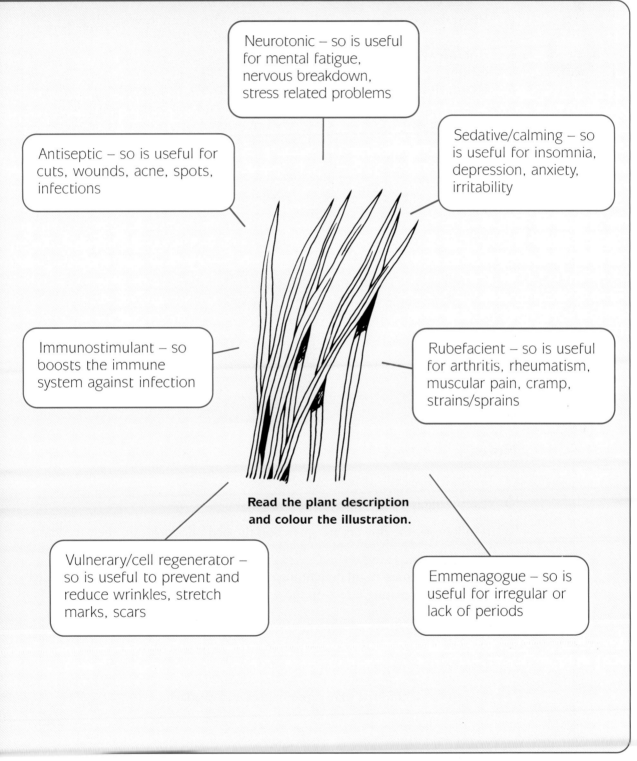

Neurotonic – so is useful for mental fatigue, nervous breakdown, stress related problems

Sedative/calming – so is useful for insomnia, depression, anxiety, irritability

Antiseptic – so is useful for cuts, wounds, acne, spots, infections

Immunostimulant – so boosts the immune system against infection

Rubefacient – so is useful for arthritis, rheumatism, muscular pain, cramp, strains/sprains

Read the plant description and colour the illustration.

Vulnerary/cell regenerator – so is useful to prevent and reduce wrinkles, stretch marks, scars

Emmenagogue – so is useful for irregular or lack of periods

CANANGA ODORATA – YLANG-YLANG

- **Plant description:** Tall tropical tree with green leaves and large mauve, pink or yellow flowers
- **Botanical family:** Annonaceae
- **Note:** Base
- **Extraction:** Steam distillation of the flowers (the yellow flowers are considered the best)
- **Production:** Originated in tropical Asia. Produced in the Philippines, Indonesia and Madagascar
- **Blends well with:** Bergamot, grapefruit, geranium, jasmine, lavender, lemon, mandarin, melissa, neroli, orange, patchouli, rose, rosewood, sandalwood, vetiver

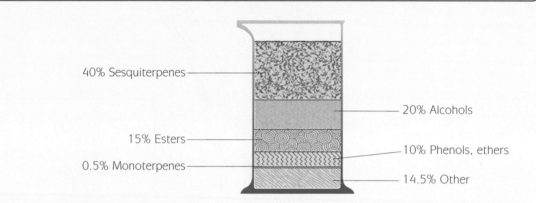

40% Sesquiterpenes

20% Alcohols

15% Esters

10% Phenols, ethers

0.5% Monoterpenes

14.5% Other

Notes

- Ylang-ylang means 'flower of flowers'.
- Ylang-ylang is a well-known aphrodisiac.
- In Indonesia, the flowers are spread on the bed of couples on their wedding night.
- In Victorian times an oil containing ylang-ylang called macassar oil was used due to its stimulating effect on the scalp and to encourage hair growth.

Caution

- Possible sensitisation in some people.
- Use in moderation as may cause nausea and headache.

Ylang-ylang

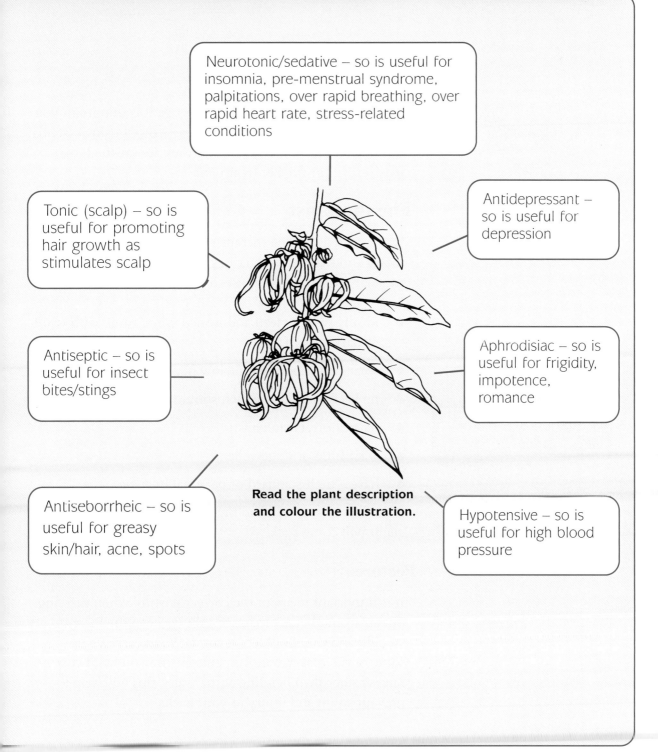

Neurotonic/sedative – so is useful for insomnia, pre-menstrual syndrome, palpitations, over rapid breathing, over rapid heart rate, stress-related conditions

Tonic (scalp) – so is useful for promoting hair growth as stimulates scalp

Antidepressant – so is useful for depression

Antiseptic – so is useful for insect bites/stings

Aphrodisiac – so is useful for frigidity, impotence, romance

Antiseborrheic – so is useful for greasy skin/hair, acne, spots

Read the plant description and colour the illustration.

Hypotensive – so is useful for high blood pressure

Giving an Aromatherapy Treatment

When giving an aromatherapy massage it is important that the treatment is professional and carried out using essential oils that suit the client's needs; if they are satisfied, they may return for further treatment.

The therapist

It is essential that the therapist presents a professional image and manner when carrying out an aromatherapy massage. An aromatherapist should:

Note

Remember to always wear a smile!

- ideally wear a clean and ironed white tunic with white or dark trousers;
- wear clean shoes with a low heel;
- tie back long hair, which should be clean;
- have short, clean nails;
- wear little or no jewellery;
- have a high standard of personal hygiene.

If the therapist gives a bad first impression it is unlikely the client will come back.

Posture

It is important to adopt the correct posture when carrying out an aromatherapy massage. Always keep the back straight and the shoulders relaxed. When carrying out some of the massage movements ensure you bend your knees rather than bending at the waist; this will help to prevent strain and injury to your back.

The client

Any jewellery, such as necklaces and earrings, should be removed from the client prior to the massage. This will prevent the jewellery accidentally being broken and will help to ensure the massage flows correctly.

If you are massaging the face, any make-up should be removed; perhaps you could ask the client to do this prior to coming. You can remove make-up with cleanser and some damp cottonwool pads, ensuring the client is not allergic to the product. Firstly pour the cleanser into your fingers and gently rub your hands together. Using the fingers, apply it to the client's neck and face. It is important not to drag the skin and to work in an upwards direction.

Cleansing the eye area

Cleansing the lips

Cleansing the face

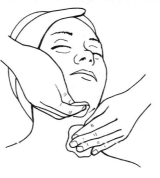
Removing cleanser

Note

Use the ring fingers to work around the eyes as they exert the least pressure.

Figure 6.1 *Cleansing the face*

The therapy room

Ensure your therapy room is clean, tidy and well presented. Ensure everything is at hand and that towels are neatly folded, the trolley neatly laid out with perhaps crystals and an attractive bowl in which to pour out the oil. You may also consider subdued lighting and relaxing music.

How long will the treatment take?

An aromatherapy massage treatment will last for about one hour and thirty minutes; this includes the facial massage and consultation. A back massage will take about twenty minutes. It is important to ensure your client is aware of how long the treatment will take.

Consultation

The consultation is an important part of the aromatherapy massage treatment and will usually last for about fifteen minutes, although the first consultation may take longer. The consultation begins with greeting the client and asking him or her to sit down. A consultation form is used to write down client information; inform the client that all information given is confidential and that the details will be securely stored. Ensuring client confidentiality will help create a trusting professional relationship between the client and therapist.

You should also look at the client's non-verbal communication, i.e. is there nervousness, but most importantly you should listen carefully to what the client has to say. The consultation is essential for the following reasons:

- It helps you to get to know the client so you can develop a good relationship with him or her.

- It allows you to find out the medical details of the client to establish if there are medical reasons (contra-indications) why the treatment should not go ahead.

- The client's expectations of the treatment can be established, which will also help to reassure a nervous client.

- The consultation will help you establish what the objectives of the client are; perhaps the client needs help with aches or pains or a stress-related condition.

- It helps you to treat the client in a holistic way, as you can find out about the lifestyle of the client; perhaps emotional factors are causing persistent headaches. Maybe the client's job involves bending the neck a great deal so is causing neck problems or perhaps heavy lifting is affecting the shoulders. If the client feels persistently tired, one cause of this is often stress and so relaxation techniques can be given.

- Make a note of points of interest discussed by the client: perhaps an exam, holiday, wedding etc. You can refer back to these points the next time you meet.

Overleaf is an example of an aromatherapy massage consultation form. You may want to design your own form so that you can use it in the future.

Note

'Contra' is a Latin word meaning 'against'. 'Indication' literally means an indication against doing the treatment.

AROMATHERAPY CONSULTATION FORM

NAME: ....

TEL NO: ....

ADDRESS: ....

....

EMAIL ADDRESS: ....

D.O.B: ....

OCCUPATION: ....

MEDICAL QUESTIONNAIRE

Do you suffer with or have you ever suffered with any of the following:

High or low blood pressure? ....

Heart condition? ....

Liver complaints (e.g. hepatitis)? ....

Epilepsy? ....

Digestive problems (e.g. irritable bowel syndrome)? ....

Recent haemorrhage? ....

Thrombosis or embolism? ....

Lumps/swellings? ....

Varicose veins? ....

Diabetes? ....

Spastic conditions (e.g. muscular spasms)? ....

Dysfunction of the nervous system (e.g. Parkinson's disease)? ....

Skin disorders/scalp infections? ....

Allergies? ....

Cuts or abrasions in the area being treated? ....

Recent operations? ....

Fluid retention (oedema)? ....

Any discomfort/pain in your body? ....

Anxiety/depression? ....

Are you pregnant? ....

Are you currently on medication? ....

Is GP referral required? Yes/No

Name of doctor: ....

Surgery address: ....

Tel no: ....

Figure 6.2 *A sample aromatherapy consultation form*

LIFESTYLE

Do you drink alcohol, and if so how often? ....

Do you smoke, and if so how many each day? ....

Do you eat healthily? ....

Do you drink plenty of fluids (water)? ....

Do you sleep well? ....

How often do you exercise? ....

What are your hobbies: how do you relax? ....

Are you going through any major life changes such as menopause, bereavement, loss of job, retirement, etc.? ....

Would you say your stress levels are: high/average/low? ....

Details if levels are high: ....

....

....

Would you say your energy levels are: high/average/poor? ....

Have you ever had any previous holistic therapy treatments? ....

....

Are you currently receiving homeopathic treatment? ....

....

Why have you come for aromatherapy massage? ....

....

....

Additional notes: (e.g. Is there any referral data from other health professionals?) ....

....

....

....

Client declaration

The information I have given regarding my medical details is accurate. I will promptly notify the therapist of any future changes to my health.

Client signature ....Date ....

Date ....

Treatment notes: ....

....

....

....

Figure 6.2 (cont.)   *A sample aromatherapy consultation form*

The aromatherapy massage treatment will involve a thorough consultation but you do not need to write out consultation forms every time the client comes to you. However, you need to find out if the client's circumstances have changed in any way since the last treatment, especially medically, and note it on his or her form.

Aromatherapy is a holistic treatment, which means the mind, body and spirit are taken into account in attempting to improve the health of an individual. This is why during the consultation clients are asked about lifestyle factors including hobbies and stress levels. If you feel a client needs to de-stress and undertake exercise you can recommend activities such as yoga and t'ai chi. Relaxation exercises and breathing techniques will also help the client relax and de-stress.

Task 6.1

List five reasons why the consultation is an important part of the aromatherapy treatment:

_____

_____

_____

_____

_____

Contra-indications

Aromatherapy is a very safe treatment, but there are certain conditions that the therapist should be aware of that may prevent treatment being carried out or require the advice of a doctor.

Table 6.1 Contra-indications to aromatherapy

Any recent fractures or sprains
Severe bruising, cuts or abrasion in treatment area
Epilepsy
Recent haemorrhage or swellings
High blood pressure/low blood pressure
Thrombosis/embolism
Diabetes
Spastic conditions
Dysfunction of the nervous system
Skin disorders/nail diseases/scalp infections
Recent operations
Varicose veins
Pregnancy
On abdomen during first two days of menstruation
Sunburn
Fever
Infectious diseases
Cancer

If, during consultation, the client informs you, for instance, that they have high blood pressure so are contra-indicated to treatment, it should be explained to the client that it is in his or her interest not to continue with treatment as it could potentially harm the client or worsen the condition.

The contra-indications listed above are now discussed in more detail.

Any recent fractures or sprains

Massage would be extremely uncomfortable for a client and could worsen the condition.

Severe bruising, cuts or abrasions in treatment area

Bruises, cuts and abrasions are localised contra-indications, which means that massage can be carried out around them, but if bruising or cuts are severe it may be wise to ask the client to return after the affected area has healed. If there is slight bleeding, ensure that a plaster covers the infected area and that you do not touch it in case of cross-infection.

Note

Do not touch anything contaminated with blood unless you have surgical gloves on. Put the item into a plastic bag and tie the top to secure it. Ensure that the bag and gloves are disposed of safely.

Epilepsy

Epilepsy is a disorder of the brain in which the patient suffers fits or convulsions. The convulsions are due to a surge of over-activity in the brain's electrical system. Usually there is no obvious cause, however, in some cases the fits are due to scars on the brain from surgery or injury. Certain essential oils are thought to trigger epileptic fits. The advice of a doctor should be sought before treatment can be carried out.

Recent haemorrhage or swellings

Haemorrhage is the term for excessive bleeding, which can be internal or external. It is advisable not to give treatment to someone who has had a recent haemorrhage because the massage may cause further haemorrhaging.

High blood pressure (HBP)

High blood pressure (hypertension) is when the blood pressure is consistently above normal. It can lead to strokes and heart attacks as the heart has to work harder to force blood through the system. High blood pressure can be caused by smoking, obesity, lack of exercise, eating too much salt, stress, too much alcohol, the contraceptive pill, pregnancy and hereditary factors.

Massage increases the blood circulation, thus possibly increasing the blood pressure, but as vasodilation (widening) of the blood vessels also occurs there could be a side-effect to massage of lowering the blood pressure, especially after a while. These effects probably counterbalance each other. Massage treatment is also relaxing, so can also be of benefit to people with high blood pressure that has been brought on by stress. Abnormal blood pressure is an important contra-indication and it is advisable to seek the doctor's advice.

Note

Advise clients suffering with HBP or LBP to get up slowly after treatment. For clients suffering with HBP ensure that the treatment is relaxing by using lots of stroking movements.

Note

Clients on antihypertensive drugs to help treat high blood pressure may suffer with postural hypotension (low blood pressure), so when they stand up after treatment they may feel light-headed and dizzy.

Low blood pressure (LBP)

Low blood pressure (hypotension) is when the blood pressure is below normal for a substantial time. Blood pressure must be sufficient to pump blood to the brain when the body is in the upright position. If it is not then the person will feel faint. It is advisable to seek the advice of a doctor before treatment.

History of thrombosis or embolism

Thrombosis is a clotting of blood found within an artery or vein. It is dangerous as it may constrict or cut off the flow of blood. If massage is carried out there is a risk that the clot may be moved or broken up and taken to the heart, lungs or brain, which could prove fatal.

Embolism is a blockage of an artery, often caused by a clot of blood, but can also be due to air, fat or bone marrow. It circulates the bloodstream until it becomes wedged somewhere in a blood vessel and blocks the flow of blood. Such a blockage may be extremely harmful. An embolism can be the cause of a stroke. Do not treat clients with thrombosis or embolism, and if there has been a history of these conditions obtain the doctor's advice.

Diabetes

Diabetes mellitus results from too little output of insulin from the pancreas gland. Insulin is needed to allow glucose (sugar) into the body's cells so the body can use it to make energy. The lack of insulin causes the sugar to build up in the blood instead. Some symptoms indicating diabetes include tiredness, an initial weight loss, and excessive thirst and urination.

People with poorly controlled diabetes may have related conditions such as high blood pressure, hardened arteries, altered sensations in limbs such as numbness, eyesight problems, poor healing of the skin and wasting of the tissues, such as the skin, which may be paper thin. It is advisable to seek the advice of the doctor before treatment.

Spastic conditions

When the muscles are in spasm, so in a state of contraction, massage could be uncomfortable to the client.

Dysfunction of the nervous system

Any dysfunction of the nervous system includes conditions such as multiple sclerosis, cerebral palsy, Parkinson's disease and motor neurone disease. The doctor's advice should be sought prior to treatment.

Skin disorders/nail diseases/scalp infections

Treatment can be given if the skin disorder, nail disease or scalp infection is not infectious, there is no bleeding or weeping and it would not cause discomfort when massaged. Otherwise the area can be worked around or the client should return when the condition has cleared.

Recent operations

If the client has had any recent operations to the area you intend to treat, especially within the last six months, it is wise not to carry out the aromatherapy massage treatment. If the operation is minor, the doctor's advice can be sought.

Varicose veins

Varicose veins are permanently dilated (widened) veins in which blood pools and causes them to swell and bulge. They are due to valves in the veins not working properly and commonly occur in the veins near the surface of the leg. A varicose vein is a local contra-indication so massage treatment can be given around the affected area.

Pregnancy

Aromatherapy treatment should not be carried out during the first three months of pregnancy. Pregnancy can lead to a variety of contra-indications so only those therapists who have a full understanding of the specific contra-indications that pregnancy can cause, and feel confident to do so, should perform any treatment on pregnant clients. Before any treatment can be carried out the client's doctor or midwife's advice should be sought.

Note

Check with your insurance company that you are insured to treat pregnant clients.

On abdomen during first two days of menstruation

The abdomen will be tender at this time so no massage should be given on the abdomen, although the rest of the body can be treated.

Cancer

It is feared that giving massage treatment to someone suffering with cancer will cause the cancer to spread through the lymphatic and circulatory systems, although there has been no evidence to support this.

Aromatherapy massage may be given to people with cancer if under medical supervision. The use of essential oils is a controversial subject. It is advised not to use essential oils on someone undergoing chemotherapy or radiotherapy as the skin may become hypersensitive to the touch and easily irritated.

Essential oils that may be beneficial to use on people with cancer include neroli, bergamot, mandarin, clary sage, rose, ylang-ylang, frankincense and sandalwood. Use the oils with care and carry out an allergy test first (see Chapter 2).

Patients taking homeopathic remedies

Some homeopaths believe that all essential oils interfere with the effects of homeopathic remedies. Other therapists believe that only the camphoraceous oils are contra-indicated. Clients should tell their homeopath that they are coming for aromatherapy treatment.

> **Note**
>
> Check with your insurance company to ensure that you are covered to give aromatherapy massage to people with cancer.

> **Note**
>
> Ask the client to obtain doctor's advice if you are ever unsure whether it is safe to give a treatment!

Research the contra-indications to aromatherapy and state the reason why aromatherapy treatment should not be given below:

Contra-indications	Why contra-indicated for treatment
Recent fractures or sprains	
Severe bruising, cuts or abrasions on treatment area	
Epilepsy	
Recent haemorrhage or swellings	
High blood pressure/low blood pressure	
Thrombosis/embolism	
Diabetes	
Spastic conditions	
Dysfunction of the nervous system	
Skin disorders/nail diseases/scalp infections	
Recent operations	
Varicose veins	
Pregnancy (first trimester)	
First two days of menstruation on abdomen	
Sunburn	
Fever	
Infectious diseases	
Cancer	

Referral letters

Referral letter to client's doctor

If clients seeking aromatherapy treatment have a contra-indication it is advisable that they obtain advice from their doctor regarding their medical condition and suitability for treatment. It is a good idea to have a standard letter, which clients can give to the doctor or post, enclosing a stamp-addressed envelope. The doctor need only sign their name to advise their patients if they think there is a medical reason why treatment should not go ahead.

Address of treatment room

Date

Dr's address

Dear Dr [*name*]

Your patient, [*name*] of [*his/her address*] has informed me that [*he/she*] is suffering with [*high blood pressure, diabetes*].

Please advise me if in your view there is any reason why your patient should not have aromatherapy treatment.
Thank you.

Yours sincerely

[*Your signature*]

[*Your name printed*]

Dr's advice
I feel [*name of client*] would/would not be suitable for having aromatherapy massage treatment.
Dr's signature .... Date........................

Figure 6.3 *A sample referral letter to a client's doctor*

Handling referral data from professional sources

If a health care professional, be it a doctor or a reflexologist etc., should refer a client to you for aromatherapy massage treatment, it is courteous to keep the professional informed of the client's progress. A progress report should include the following information:

- The client's name, who referred the client and his or her reason for coming for aromatherapy massage treatment.

- How the client is progressing.

- The treatment plan for the future.

A brief letter can be written reporting the progress of a client, an example of which follows overleaf.

Note

Ensure you have the client's permission before sending the progress report.

Note

Doctors often do not know what an aromatherapy massage treatment entails and therefore cannot give permission as such for treatment to go ahead; they can only advise their patients. Doctors' insurance does not cover them for giving permission or consent regarding holistic therapy treatments.

Clinic name, address and telephone number

Dear [*name of professional*]

Thank you for recommending [*client's name*] to come to me for aromatherapy massage treatment. I am writing to inform you of her progress.

[*Client's name*] has been having regular weekly treatments for the past month. She is feeling less anxious and irritable and has also suffered with fewer headaches since treatment began. [*Client's name*] feels that the treatments have helped her to de-stress and relax.

We are to continue her treatments for two more weeks and she will return to me on a monthly basis.

If you require further information please do not hesitate to contact me.

Yours sincerely

[*Your name and position*]

Figure 6.4 *A sample referral letter of progress to a health professional*

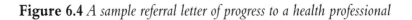

Preparing a treatment plan

A treatment plan will ensure you have a plan of action, which will help you and your client reach your objectives. The plan will include the client's expectations of the treatment, therefore helping to ensure client satisfaction.

At any time you can change your treatment plan to suit you and your client. You can also monitor progress to see if changes are needed in any way.

How often should clients come for treatment?

You will need to discuss how often the treatment should be carried out with your clients. It will depend on the clients' finances, time and reasons for coming. If clients have come for relaxation maybe they could attend once every two weeks; if they have a particular condition that needs treating you could advise them coming for treatment once a week for six weeks. Emphasise to your clients the importance of regular treatments to maintain the long-term benefits.

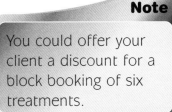

Note

You could offer your client a discount for a block booking of six treatments.

Course of treatments

If a client books a course of aromatherapy treatments it may be a good idea to review and evaluate your choice of essential oils each time the treatment is given. If certain essential oils have proved beneficial it would be advisable to keep using the same oils or maybe make slight adjustments.

Note

Why not write to your client's husband or wife a couple of weeks before your client's birthday and ask if he or she would like to purchase a voucher for an aromatherapy massage treatment?

```
┌─────────────────────────────────────────────────────────────────────────┐
│  Treatment plan                                                           │
├───────────────────────────────────────────────────────────────────────── │
│                                                                           │
│  Client name ..................Ms M. Lucas..........  Date of treatment...21 July 2____ │
│  Treatment given ..........Aromatherapy massage....................................... │
│                                                                           │
│  What are the client's expectations of treatment?                         │
│                                                                           │
│  *   To be relaxed                                                        │
│  *   To help with eczema                                                  │
│  *   To help with pre-menstrual syndrome.                                 │
│                                                                           │
│  What are the treatment objectives?                                       │
│                                                                           │
│  *   To help relax client                                                 │
│  *   To choose essential oils that are excellent for stress and irritability, │
│      that will help with all conditions                                   │
│  *   To use oils helpful for eczema.                                      │
│                                                                           │
│  Essential oils chosen and no. of drops used:                             │
│   Lavender and bergamot, 5 drops of each                                  │
│  .......................................................................  │
│                                                                           │
│  Carrier oil used and amount:                                             │
│   Almond oil, 20 ml                                                       │
│  .......................................................................  │
├───────────────────────────────────────────────────────────────────────── │
│                                                                           │
│  Recommended frequency of treatment...................................... │
│  Weekly treatments for a period of six weeks (this can be changed at a later date) │
├───────────────────────────────────────────────────────────────────────── │
│                                                                           │
│  Additional notes:                                                        │
│                                                                           │
│  *   Particular areas of tension in body that need specific massage.      │
│  *   Any fluid retention.                                                 │
│  *   Skin type (if treating the skin on the face).                        │
│  *   Particular massage movements enjoyed by client.                      │
│  *   Any special needs, maybe need help on to couch.                      │
│  *   Outcome of treatment, was it effective?                              │
│  *   Any problems that arise.                                             │
│                                                                           │
└─────────────────────────────────────────────────────────────────────────┘
```

Figure 6.5 *A sample treatment plan*

Aftercare advice

It is important for the client to follow aftercare advice so that the full benefits of the treatment can be gained. Give the following advice after the treatment has been completed.

- Advise the client not to have a shower/bath or sauna for 24 hours – this will allow thorough penetration of the essential oils. Many essential oils take up to an hour to absorb through the skin.

- The client should not sunbathe or use sunbeds for 24 hours – if it is phototoxic, the carrier or essential oil may cause the skin to burn.

- The client should be encouraged to rest and relax after the treatment, to ensure the body is able to heal itself sufficiently.

- Encourage the client to drink plenty of water (mineral or tap) or herbal teas to help speed up the removal of toxins from the body.

- Coffee, tea and cola should be avoided as they contain caffeine. Caffeine is a stimulant to the body, so will not help the client to relax.

- Clients should not smoke or drink alcohol for about 24 hours, as the treatment is a detoxifying one, and smoking and drinking will reintroduce toxins into the body.

- Heavy meals should be avoided after treatment as blood is diverted to the gut to help with the digestion of the food and this will divert energy away from the healing processes. Light meals such as fruit and vegetables make ideal snacks.

- It may be wise to ask clients to wait for about ten minutes after the treatment before driving home, especially if they feel sleepy.

- It is important that the client relaxes after the aromatherapy treatment. Some helpful relaxation exercise techniques are given in Chapter 7, which could be described to the client.

Study the information given on aftercare advice to enable you to answer the questions below.

Why should a client not shower/bath or sauna for 24 hours after treatment?

_____

_____

Why should a client not sunbathe or use sunbeds for 24 hours?

_____

_____

Why should a client rest and relax after treatment?

_____

_____

Why should a client drink lots of water after treatment?

_____

_____

Why should a client avoid coffee, tea and cola after treatment?

_____

_____

Why should a client not drink alcohol or smoke cigarettes after treatment?

_____

_____

What dietary advice would you give your client after treatment?

_____

_____

Why should a client wait a little while after treatment before driving home?

_____

_____

Contra-actions (healing crises)

After an aromatherapy massage a client will usually feel relaxed and reap the benefits of the treatment, but occasionally a client may experience a contra-action, also called a healing crisis. A contra-action is a reaction that may happen during or after the aromatherapy massage treatment is given.

During treatment

♦ A client may experience aching or soreness in the muscles; this is due to the release of toxins.

♦ Tiredness can also be due to the release of toxins. The body will need to rest to enable its healing energies to carry out its work effectively. After the tiredness has disappeared the client should feel refreshed and full of energy!

♦ A heightened emotional state – your client may feel a little emotional, maybe even tearful. It is a good way for the client to release tension.

After treatment

Occasionally a client may report any of the following reactions 24–48 hours after treatment.

♦ headache

♦ dizziness or nausea

♦ disrupted sleeping pattern

♦ increased release of mucus in the nose or mouth

♦ excessive urination

♦ increase in bowel movements

♦ erythema

♦ irritation

♦ fatigue

♦ hyperactivity

- change of appetite
- skin changes.

These reactions are mainly due to toxins being released from the body, as the body is rebalancing and cleansing itself.

Home use blends

To maintain the benefits of the aromatherapy massage a client may wish to purchase a blend of oils for home use. If a client has enjoyed a particular mix and it has proved successful the therapist can mix up a similar blend for home use. Use one drop of essential oil for every 5 ml of carrier oil. You can discuss the best method of application with your client. Ensure you write down details of the oils that have been blended in case the client experiences any problems.

A blended oil will last for three months but if mixed with 10 per cent wheatgerm it will last for six months.

Self-test questions

Write your answers to the questions below, then check against the sample answers on the web site (www.saloneducation.co.uk).

1. Why is it important for the therapist to be well presented and to have a professional attitude?

_____

_____

_____

2. Why must particular attention be paid to personal and general hygiene when treating clients?

   _____

   _____

   _____

3. Why is it important to be aware of the client's body language (perhaps they are nervous) and to react positively towards them?

   _____

   _____

   _____

4. How would you reassure a nervous client about the aromatherapy massage treatment?

   _____

   _____

   _____

5. List six contra-indications to aromatherapy treatment.

   _____

   _____

   _____

   _____

   _____

   _____

6. If, during the consultation, your client informs you that he or she has high blood pressure, what action would you take?

    _____

    _____

    _____

7. If, during the consultation, your client informs you of a bruise on his or her arm, how would you modify the massage?

    _____

    _____

    _____

8. What is the purpose of a doctor's referral letter?

    _____

    _____

    _____

9. Why is it important to establish the reasons the client has come to you and his or her expectations during the consultation?

    _____

    _____

    _____

10. Why is it important that the client record card is clearly written and that all the information is accurate and regularly updated?

    _____

    _____

    _____

11. What aftercare advice should be given to the client after aromatherapy treatment?

   _____

   _____

   _____

   _____

   _____

12. Name five contra-actions that may occur 24–48 hours after aromatherapy treatment.

   _____

   _____

   _____

   _____

   _____

   _____

   _____

   _____

13. When mixing up a home blend for a client what proportions of essential and carrier oils would you use?

   _____

   _____

Massage movements and their effects

When carrying out aromatherapy massage you will use different types of massage movements called effleurage, petrissage, neuromuscular and lymphatic drainage.

Effleurage

Effleurage movements always begin and end the massage on each area. The effleurage movement can be superficial (using light pressure) or deep, using slightly deeper pressure. These movements must always follow the direction of venous return (blood in veins back to the heart) and also in the direction of lymphatic drainage towards a group of lymph nodes. The hands stay in contact with the body during the return stroke.

Uses of effleurage

◊ To spread the oil so that the area being massaged is lubricated.

◊ Introduces the therapist's hands.

◊ To warm up the area so deeper massage movements can be used.

◊ Links massage movements together, so that the massage flows.

◊ Relaxes the receiver.

Effects of effleurage

- Improves the blood and lymphatic circulation.

- Aids desquamation (removal of dead skin cells), so the skin will look healthier and feel smoother.

- Soothes nerve endings, therefore inducing relaxation.

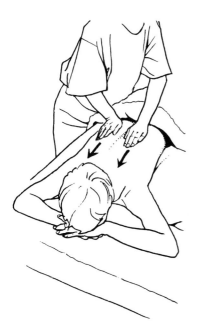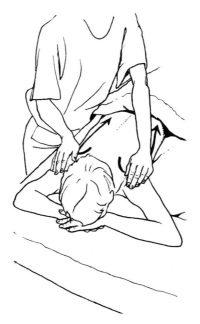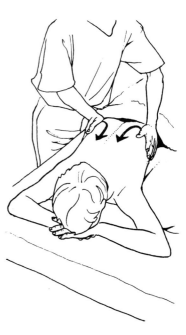

Figure 7.1 *Effleurage to the back*

Petrissage

Petrissage movements are deeper techniques in which soft tissues such as muscles are squeezed together and compressed. These movements either press the muscle on to the bone, or lift the muscle away from the bone. The whole hand, fingers or thumbs can be used.

Note

Petrissage is a French word meaning 'kneading'.

There are different types of petrissage movements, which include the following:

- ◆ *Picking up* – the tissues are picked up and lifted away from the bone and then released, using one or both hands.

- ◆ *Kneading* – the muscle is pressed on to the bone using firm movements with the palms of one hand or both hands, or with the pads of the fingers or thumbs.

Uses of petrissage

- ◆ To stimulate sluggish blood circulation.
- ◆ To aid lymphatic drainage.
- ◆ To improve condition of skin and hair.
- ◆ To ease muscular tension.

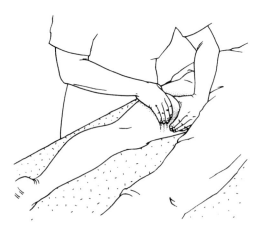

Figure 7.2 *Petrissage to the back of leg and thigh*

Effects of petrissage

Note

Most massage movements will be a type of petrissage.

- ◆ Blood and lymphatic circulation is increased encouraging fresh oxygen and nutrients to be delivered to the tissues (such as the muscles and skin) and an increased removal of waste products.
- ◆ Erythema (redness) is produced on the skin.
- ◆ The elimination of toxins from the body is speeded up.
- ◆ The secretion of sebum is increased, so moisturising skin and hair.

Neuromuscular massage

Neuromuscular (means nerve–muscle) massage is a Western massage developed and used in the USA. Its purpose is to treat areas of tension or tension nodules. Neuromuscular techniques involve using the pads of the thumbs and/or fingers to apply deep and firm massage to the nerves, muscles, tendons and ligaments. Thumbs are often used as they apply more pressure. Arms are generally kept straight so that the therapist can use the body weight to add depth. The pressure may be held for up to a minute and repeated.

Neuromuscular massage not only uses pressures on a specific point but also uses different massage movements with the fingers and thumbs such as circling, four finger stroking, effleurage away from the spine and petrissage along nerve pathways.

Each spinal nerve divides into branches, forming groups of nerves called plexuses. An example of a plexus is the brachial plexus, which supplies the whole of the shoulders and arms. A painful area of the body, such as in a muscle, may be traced back to one of the main spinal nerves. Sometimes the pain is referred so the origin of the pain may be within a spinal nerve and working that specific spinal nerve will help to ease the pain.

Another type of neuromuscular technique involves working on specific motor points of muscles, which are deeply massaged with the fingertips.

Note

Neuromuscular techniques can be incorporated into the general body massage routine.

Note

A motor point is where the nerve enters the belly of the muscle. Pressure is applied at this area on a painful or weak muscle, but only for about ten seconds.

This neuromuscular massage may cause discomfort for the client but will help to clear the nerve pathways so help the area of pain in the body.

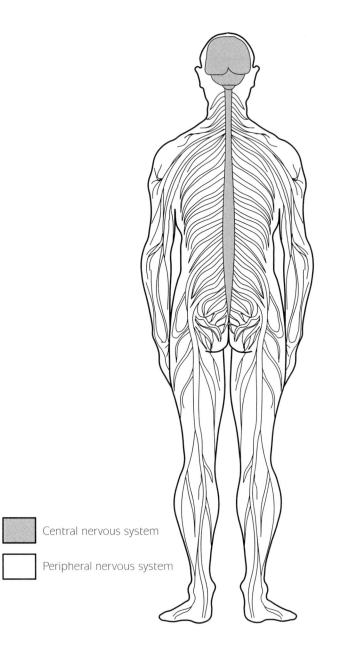

Central nervous system

Peripheral nervous system

Figure 7.3 *Nerve pathways of the body*

Effects of neuromuscular massage

- Relieves pain.

- Increases blood circulation.

- Increases endorphin output (the body's own mood-lifting and pain-relieving hormones).

- Relieves congestion in nerve pathways.

Lymphatic drainage

This is a superficial massage that aids lymphatic drainage. It is thought that by applying pressure to superficial lymph vessels it will have an effect on the deeper lymph vessels. However, all massage will stimulate the lymphatic flow and so aid drainage. Clients with areas of oedema (fluid retention), commonly seen around the ankles, will benefit from this type of massage as the lymphatic drainage techniques will help to reduce puffiness and remove excess fluid from the affected area.

The lymphatic drainage massage should be slow and rhythmic. It consists of using the tips of fingers or thumbs and applying varying pressures according to the area being treated, although deep pressure is not required. Long, gentle strokes will help to push lymph gently towards the nearest lymph gland.

Effects of lymphatic drainage

- Increases lymphatic circulation.

- Increases blood circulation.

- Removes build-up of excess fluid.

Note

To help with fluid retention around the ankles, elevate the legs to a maximum of 45 degrees while the client is lying on the couch.

State three effects of each massage movement below.

Form of massage movements	Three effects of the massage movement
Effleurage	_____
	_____
	_____
Petrissage	_____
	_____
	_____
Neuromuscular	_____
	_____
	_____
Lymphatic drainage	_____
	_____
	_____

Acupressure points/pressures

Acupressure is an ancient Chinese healing method. It involves applying pressures with fingers or thumbs to certain points of the body to aid the smooth flow of energy, known as chi. Chi, sometimes known as qi or ki, is vital as it supports, nourishes and protects the emotional and physical well being. Chi is said to pass through twelve main channels or meridians in the body. If chi becomes blocked, for example by negative thoughts, it may cause stress and ill health. By stimulating relevant points acupressure can help restore balance by releasing blocked energy and relieve muscular tensions and also aid the circulation of the blood. Acupressure is helpful to relieve pain and promote good health.

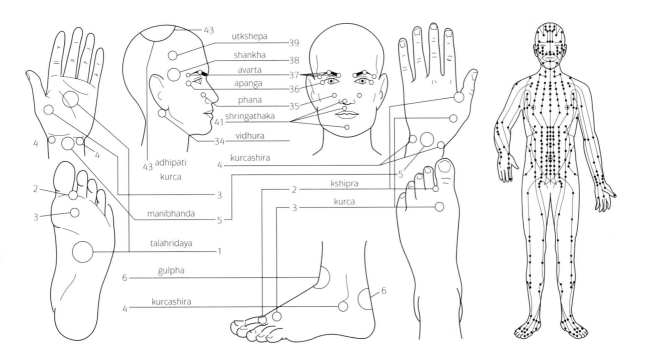

Figure 7.4 *Meridians of the body (from Pitman and McKenzie, Reflexology: A Practical Approach, Nelson Thornes, p.xiv)*

Acupressure points

Large intestine meridian

1. Press the area between the finger and thumb for five seconds, three times. This is useful for headaches, neck problems, toothache and constipation.

2. Bend the arm at a right angle and press at the end of the crease in elbow. Press for five seconds, three times, ensuring that both arms are worked. This is useful for arm pains, headaches, fever and diarrhoea.

Gall bladder meridian

3. Press the area below the knee and in front of the bony protrusion on the side of the leg. Press for five seconds, three times. This is useful for knee problems, aiding digestion, headaches and tension.

Kidney meridian

4. Press the area half way between the tip of the anklebone and the Achilles' tendon. Press for five seconds, three times and work both feet. This is useful for kidney problems, lower back pain, menstrual problems and fluid retention.

Note

Acupressure is not advisable if the client is pregnant, has an infection or is suffering from a serious health disorder.

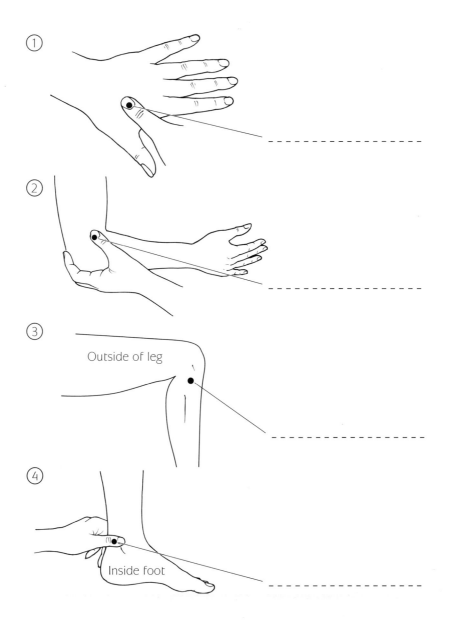

Figure 7.5 *Acupressure points to large intestine, gall bladder and kidney meridians*

Chakras and auras

Chakras

Part of traditional Indian belief is that the body is divided into chakras. When giving an aromatherapy treatment you will be working over chakras. The body has seven major chakras: crown (7); brow (third eye) (6); throat (5); heart (4); solar plexus (3), hara (sacral) (2); and base (root) (1). Minor chakras are also found in the feet, palms of the hands and at joints.

Task 7.2

Name the chakras in the diagram, using the information above.

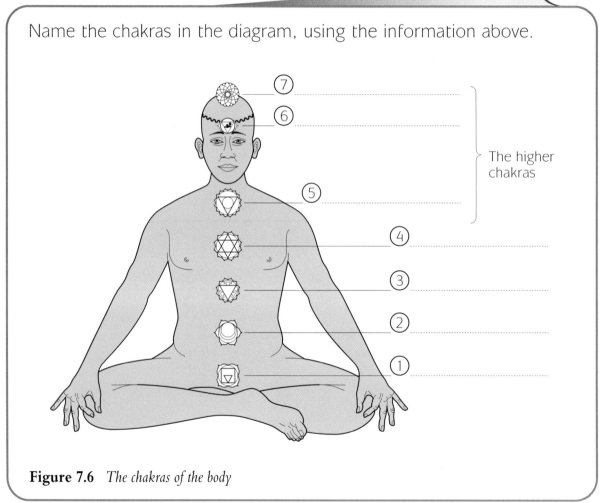

Figure 7.6 *The chakras of the body*

The chakras are centres of energy located about 3 cm (1 in) away from the body that ideally spin in a clockwise direction. To ensure health, all of the chakras need to be open, unblocked and in balance with each other. When the chakras lose their ability to work harmoniously with each other they become unbalanced.

Imbalances or blockages can be eased or corrected by contact with an energy that nourishes or vibrates at a frequency beneficial to the chakra. To help rebalance these chakras the hands can be placed over them to help the energy flow freely. Balancing means helping a chakra to achieve proper functioning so that it is not too open or closed. When in a balanced state, a person can remain calm and centred in any situation. When out of balance, people tend to withdraw, or feel overwhelmed, or lose control of their emotions.

Auras

Energy from the universe, for example the sun and earth, passes through chakras and travels through invisible channels in the body called meridians and then passes into the body's cells. The meridians therefore connect the aura and chakras with the physical body. Energy that is not required by the cells will pass out of the body through the chakras and the pores of the skin creating an aura. The aura is an energy field that surrounds the physical body. The layer found directly to the outside of our body is called the ethereal body.

The aura is made up of levels of energy called the subtle bodies. In a healthy person it makes an egg shape around the whole body and for most people it extends about 1 m (3 ft) from the body. The more healthy an individual the further the aura will extend, and the more vibrant and colourful it will be. It is said great leaders from the past had auras that extended for miles, which may explain why they had so many followers! The aura is said to be weakened by poor diet, lack of exercise, stress, lack of rest, alcohol, drugs and tobacco.

Note

Animals and plants have auras too!

The human energy field can absorb the energies of plants, flowers, trees, animals and from the earth too. Sitting under a willow tree for about ten minutes can help to alleviate a headache and pine trees are very cleansing to the aura as they absorb negative emotions.

Note

The aura expands with positive thoughts and feelings such as joy and happiness, and it contracts with negative feelings such as fear or hatred.

Healthy breathing

For most people normal, everyday breathing tends to be shallow and rapid. It mostly involves the chest expanding out and then relaxing inwards. Deep breathing for relaxation is slow and deep; it involves using the diaphragm and comes from the abdomen. Breathing, when done correctly, requires a person to inhale slowly through the nose and exhale out through the mouth; this prevents the throat from becoming dry. As air is inhaled the stomach should be allowed to move outwards. The diaphragm is pulled downwards causing the lungs to draw in air to fill the space. The diaphragm will then relax causing air to be expelled from the lungs and so we breathe out.

Slow, deep and rhythmic breathing triggers a relaxation response in the body. Some of these changes include a slower heart rate, muscular relaxation and a feeling of calmness. Relaxation exercises will also trigger a relaxation response in the body.

Breathing exercise

1. Stand with back straight and feet slightly apart. Inhale slowly and deeply through the nose, thinking about bringing the breath into the abdomen and at the same time raise the arms up and backwards over the head.

2. Momentarily hold the breath and then allow the arms and trunk to fall forwards. (Ensure knees are bent to prevent any strain.) At the same time, breathe out, creating a 'Ha' sound.

3. Breathe in slowly and raise the body into a standing position. Repeat the exercise two times.

Meditation

Meditation involves calming the mind, and will help with deep and clear thought, and so aid concentration. It helps to relax tense muscles, lower blood pressure and regulate the breathing rate. Ensure the client is relaxed, warm and comfortable.

There are different ways to meditate. One method involves concentrating on either a candle flame, a mark on the wall, breathing or words such as 'relax' or 'calm'. Thoughts may come, acknowledge them and let them pass and continue to meditate.

During meditation a mantra, meaning speech, can help to focus the mind. The sound 'om' is often used and can be repeated with every exhalation. Practise meditating for about ten minutes every day. Short and occasional meditating should be without risk. Prolonged meditating may need guidance.

Note

Driving is not recommended immediately after meditation.

Meditative breathing exercise

This simple meditative breathing exercise will help to promote calm breathing.

1. Slowly breathe in and out through the nose. Concentrate on producing a long, deep, smooth exhalation. You will naturally inhale. Allow your breathing to settle into a smooth, regular rhythm.

2. Sit comfortably with the eyes closed. Visualise your thoughts as many bubbles and imagine all the bubbles floating away. You feel very warm and relaxed.

3. Try to remain focused on your breathing. If other thoughts appear, acknowledge them and then let them float away in bubbles and again concentrate on your breathing.

4. You will feel calm and relaxed. Practise this exercise for about ten minutes every day.

Relaxation exercises

Relaxation exercises can be given to a client who is feeling stressed or anxious.

Relaxation exercise 1

Note

Take in a deep breath as you carry out each hold and release exercise.

Either sit or lie down and ensure you are comfortable. Clench both hands into fist shapes, hold for about five seconds and release. Now tense the muscles in the arms, hold for about five seconds and release. Tense the muscles in the face, hold and then release, tense the muscles of the chest, upper back, abdomen and lower back. Work through the whole body, tightening the muscles until the muscles of all parts of the body have been clenched and released.

This exercise should be repeated twice. It is good technique for releasing tension from muscles and so can help with headaches, aches and pains. It is excellent for relaxing the whole body.

Relaxation exercise 2

Note

It is estimated that 90% of what we worry about never actually happens.

Close your eyes and take several deep breaths. Begin releasing tension in the neck by rolling the head slowly from side to side. Allow tension to drain from the head, face and neck like melting wax. Feel the tension flowing out of the chest and arms. Continue this relaxation exercise, working the upper body, then the stomach, lower back and buttocks. Most of the body should now be feeling heavy and relaxed.

Remove any tension from the legs continuing to breathe slowly. Imagine your legs are heavy and relaxed. Visualise the flow of tension running down the calves. Now, concentrate on your feet and think about how they feel. Imagine the tension and pressure of walking flowing out of the feet.

Now imagine a white, warm, healing light penetrating the top of your head and flowing through the body, down your arms and legs and out through the hands and feet, taking away all tension and troubling thoughts. The warm light is freely flowing to heal and relax the body.

Visualisation

Visualisation is a powerful tool for helping to de-stress and relax both you and your client. Ensure you are comfortable and warm and then close your eyes.

Healing sanctuary

Imagine yourself walking along a country lane on a beautiful, warm day. You are feeling very happy and safe. You see a hot air balloon in a nearby field. As you reach the field you see a wooden gate. You open the gate and walk towards the balloon.

In this field you are only allowed to think of positive, happy thoughts, so you have to empty all of your problems and negative thoughts into the balloon's basket. When you have finished, the balloon and your problems float away into the distance until it is no longer visible.

Now you look over to the other side of the field and see a wall of ivy. You walk up to it and use your hands to part the ivy, and then walk inside. This place is your private healing sanctuary. You can picture anything you like such as a room, cave, beach etc., as long as you find it beautiful, calming and relaxing.

Stay there until you feel you have had enough healing and then walk back through the ivy, then through the field. Ensure you close the gate behind you and then walk back down the country lane…

This visualisation would be an excellent way to prepare and ground you prior to giving an aromatherapy massage.

Case studies

You may be required to carry out case studies and write up your treatments and submit them as part of your course. The following case study guidelines will help you.

Consultation

Carry out a consultation using a consultation form and write a summary to include the following.

◆ Information about client's lifestyle and any health considerations, e.g. varicose veins.

- Information about this client's expectations – is the objective to relieve stress, relax or uplift them?

- A treatment plan and cross-reference chart for the client.

Select and blend oils

- Which essential oils and carrier oils were used? Discuss the reasons for choosing them.

- How much essential oil and carrier oil did you use?

Massage treatment

- Did you have to change the massage treatment in any way (for example, perhaps your client is elderly and you could only massage certain areas of the body).

- Did the client suffer with fluid retention so were specific lymphatic drainage massage movements used?

- Did you use neuromuscular massage movements? If so, why?

- Were there any areas of tension in the body that needed specific work?

Effectiveness of the treatment

- Was the treatment effective? How did your client feel?

- Were there any contra-actions?

- Do you think you could have improved the treatment? If so, what would you have done differently?

- What aftercare advice did you give?

- Did you give breathing or relaxation exercises?

Next treatment

- When the client visits you again ask how he or she felt after the last treatment.

- Was the treatment beneficial?

- Did the client experience any contra-actions?

- Has the client's health altered in any way?

- Have you made any changes to the treatment plan?

On the final treatment, write a conclusion summing up the treatments and the effectiveness of them.

Case study example

Abigail is married with one child and works as a sales assistant. Her job is fairly stressful and requires quite a lot of lifting. Consequently she often complains of aches and pains, especially in her back. She finds that she becomes very irritable before her periods and also suffers with fluid retention. She also suffers with a mild case of psoriasis on her knees and elbows.

TREATMENT PLAN

Client name .....*Ms A. Turner*...................   **Date of treatment** ...*2 June 2___*...

Treatment given ....*Aromatherapy*...

What are the client's expectations of treatment?

*   *To be relaxed.*
*   *To help ease aches and pains in her back.*
*   *To help with PMS.*
*   *To help with psoriasis.*

What are the treatment objectives?

*   *To help relieve muscular tension in her back.*
*   *To relax and de-stress the client.*
*   *To help with symptoms associated with PMS.*
*   *To use massage movements to help lymphatic drainage, therefore draining toxins and excess fluid to help with fluid retention.*
*   *To treat psoriasis.*

	CONDITION 1 **Muscular tension**	CONDITION 2 **Psoriasis**	CONDITION 3 **Pre-menstrual syndrome**
Top note	Basil, eucalyptus, thyme, lemon	Bergamot	Clary sage, bergamot
Middle note	Black pepper, juniper, lavender, rosemary, chamomile, marjoram	Chamomile, geranium, lavender, juniper, carrot seed melissa	Geranium, lavender, chamomile,
Base note	Ginger, clove	Sandalwood	Rose, neroli, rosewood

Essential oils chosen and amount used

Top note – Bergamot

Middle note – Lavender, chamomile

I have decided to use bergamot as it is useful for the irritability experienced during pre-menstrual syndrome and is excellent for skin conditions such as psoriasis. Lavender and chamomile are helpful for all three conditions.

Carrier oil chosen and amount used: *Sweet almond (20 ml)*

Any special needs? *None*

Recommended frequency of treatment: *Client will return for treatment every two weeks for the next three months.*

Additional notes:

Abigail was suffering with fluid retention around the ankles so I suggested elevating the legs for about ten minutes and after that carried out lymphatic drainage strokes to help with this condition.

I felt some knots in her shoulder area and used petrissage techniques to help disperse them. She thoroughly enjoyed the back massage but was not so keen on the facial massage. Next time I will spend longer on the back and shorten the time on the face. I used some neuromuscular techniques on her lower back to help with her muscular tension. I took care to avoid the kidney area. After the massage I left Abigail to rest for ten minutes. I gave her aftercare advice and booked the next appointment.

Summary

Abigail remarked how much better her back felt and how relaxed she was. She looked forward to the next massage. She had no contra-actions during or directly after the massage. I feel the treatment went well but I took far too long and so it would not have been cost-effective if I had charged.

Figure 7.7 (cont.) *An example of a treatment plan*

Note

On the next treatment you will need to find out if your case study experienced any contra-actions such as headaches or nausea and if the client's health details have changed in any way.

Self-test questions

Write your answers to the questions below, then check against the sample answers on the web site (www.saloneducation.co.uk).

1. List three types of massage.

_____

_____

_____

2. What is acupressure?

_____

_____

_____

_____

_____

3. Give a brief description of chakras and auras.

_____

_____

_____

_____

_____

4. What are the benefits of breathing and relaxation exercises?

_____

_____

_____

The following legislation, standards and advice on good practice ensure that the therapist carries out the treatment safely and professionally. Legislation must be followed to protect you and your client from injury.

Legislation and standards relating to aromatherapy treatment

It is important to understand the health, safety and hygiene regulations relating to aromatherapy. Aromatherapists need to be aware of the following legislation and guidelines.

Health and Safety at Work Act 1974

The Health and Safety at Work Act aims to ensure that employers and employees maintain high standards of health and safety in the workplace.

If an employer has more than five employees, the workplace must have a health and safety policy, of which all staff must be aware.

Employers and employees have responsibilities under this Act. Employers must ensure that:

- the workplace does not pose a risk to the health and safety of employees and clients;
- all equipment is safe and has regular checks;
- there must be a safe system of cash handling, such as when taking money to the bank;

staff are aware of safety procedures in the workplace, and have the necessary information, instruction and training.

Employees' responsibilities are to:

- follow the health and safety policy;
- read the hazards warning labels on containers and follow the advice;
- report any potential hazard such as glass breakage or spillage of chemicals to the relevant person in the workplace.

Task 8.1

When you spot a hazard or error in the picture below draw a circle around it. There are quite a few!

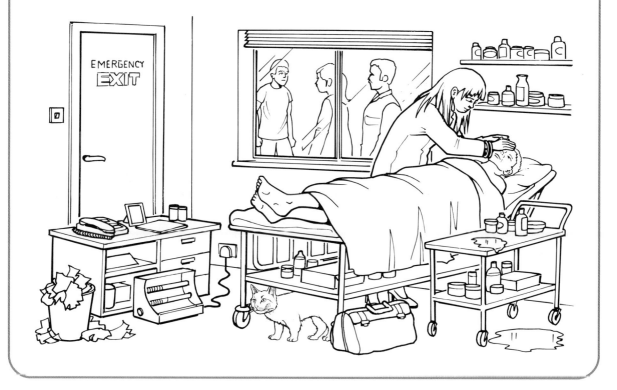

Figure 8.1 *The working environment*

Health and Safety (First Aid) Regulations 1981

A place of work must have a first aid box containing plasters, bandages, wound dressings, safety pins, eyepads and cleaning wipes.

When first aid is carried out, information such as the patient's name, date, place, time, events, any injury and treatment/advice given must be recorded.

Fire Precautions Act 1971

This Act states that all staff must be trained in fire and emergency evacuation procedure and the premises must have fire escapes.

- There must be adequate fire fighting equipment in good working order.

- Clearly marked fire exit doors should remain unlocked and must not be obstructed.

- Smoke alarms must be used.

- All staff must be trained in fire drill procedures and information regarding procedures should be displayed at the workplace.

Fire extinguishers

Fire extinguishers are colour coded for different types of fire. The table states the colour, contents and for what type of fire the extinguishers are used.

Table 8.1 Fire extinguishers

Colour	Contents of fire extinguisher	Type of fire it is used for
Red (water)	Water	Wood, paper, clothing and plastics
Blue (dry powder)	Dry powder	Electrical fires, oils, alcohols, solvents, paint; flammable liquids and gases (not on chip or fat pan fires)
Cream (foam)	Foam	Flammable liquids (not on electrical fires)
Black (CO_2)	Carbon dioxide (CO_2)	For use on electrical fires but switch off electrical supply first; grease, fats, oils, paint, flammable liquids (not on chip or fat pan fires)
Green (vaporising liquids)	Vaporising liquids	Electrical fires, flammable liquids

Note

In the future all fire extinguishers will be coloured red except for a patch or band of colour indicating the contents of the fire extinguisher.

Fire blankets are used to put out fires such as chip pan fires. The blanket covers the fire and helps prevent oxygen from fuelling the flames and so the fire is put out.

Control of Substances Hazardous to Health (COSHH) 1999

COSHH covers substances that can cause ill health. Hazardous substances such as essential oils must be used and stored away safely. All containers that contain potentially harmful chemicals must be clearly labelled. Manufacturers often give safety information regarding their products.

Corrosive

Oxidising

Toxic

Harmful irritant

Highly flammable

Explosive

Figure 8.2 *Hazard symbols*

Electricity at Work Regulations 1990

These Regulations are concerned with safety while using electricity. Any electrical equipment must be checked regularly to ensure it is safe. All checks should be listed in a record book and would be important evidence in case of any legal action.

Reporting of Injuries, Diseases and Dangerous Occurrences Regulations (RIDDOR) 1995

Minor accidents should be entered into a record book, stating what occurred and what action was taken. Ideally all concerned should sign. If, as a result of an accident at work, anyone is off work for more than three days, or someone is seriously injured, has a type of occupational disease certified by the doctor, or even dies, then the employer should send a report to the local authority environmental health department as soon as possible.

Local Government (Miscellaneous Provisions) Act 1982

By-laws are laws made by your local council and are primarily concerned with hygiene practice. Different councils around the country will have different by-laws. You will probably find there is not a by-law relating to aromatherapy treatment in your area. However, advice can be sought by contacting your local environmental health officer.

Industry Codes of Practice for Hygiene in Salons and Clinics

Vocational Training Charitable Trust in association with the Federation of Holistic Therapists publishes the code of practice. The code of practice is concerned with hygiene in the salon and gives guidelines for the therapist. Local by-laws also contain these guidelines to ensure good hygienic practice and avoid cross-infection.

Industry Code of Ethics

Under the Industry Code of Ethics a professional aromatherapist must ensure the following:

◆ All aspects of health, safety and hygiene legislation should be adhered to and the therapist should be adequately insured.

◆ The best possible treatment should be given to the client.

- The client must be respected and dignity maintained at all times.

- Never claim to cure a condition.

- Do not treat a client who is contra-indicated to treatment.

- All clients must be treated in a professional manner despite their colour, sex or religion.

- All information given, written or verbal, must be confidential and should not be disclosed to anyone without written permission, except when required to do so by law.

- Records of treatments carried out should be up to date and complete.

- Further training should be undertaken to enhance skills.

- The practitioner should be a member of a professional aromatherapy association.

Performing rights

Some therapists like to play relaxing music while giving a treatment. Any music played in waiting or treatment rooms is termed a public performance. If you play music you may need to purchase a licence from Phonographic Performance Ltd (PPL) or from the Performing Right Society (PRS). These organisations collect the licence fees and give money to the performer and record companies. If you do not buy a licence legal action may be taken against you.

However, many composers of music are not members of the PPL or PRS so no fee will need to be paid. To find out if you will need a licence contact the supplier of the music.

Data Protection Act 1998

Any information about an individual such as a client that is stored on to a computer must be registered with the data protection register. This Act ensures that this information is used by the therapist only and not given to anyone else without the client's permission. This Act does not apply to records stored manually yet, such as record cards stored in boxes, although certain manual records are being brought within data protection rules for the first time, but this applies to personal data held in structured manual files. This would affect an aromatherapist working within the health sector.

The Consumer Protection Act 1987

This Act provides the customer with protection when purchasing goods or services to ensure that products are safe for use on the client during the treatment, or are safe to be sold as a retail product.

In the past if a person was injured they had to prove that the manufacturer was negligent before they could sue for damages. This Act removed the need to prove negligence. A customer can sue a supplier without having to prove the supplier was negligent.

If you decide to label your own aromatherapy products you should refer to the Cosmetic Products (Safety) Regulations 1996. A guide to these regulations and other information related to aromatherapy should be available at your local library or The Stationery Office.

Trade Descriptions Acts 1968 and 1972

A description of a product or service, either spoken or written, must be accurate. It is illegal to use false or misleading descriptions to sell, for example to state a product can cure a skin disorder, if this information is inaccurate.

Note

A product has to be offered for sale at its full price for at least 28 days before a reduced price can be offered.

Sale and Supply of Goods Act 1994 (replaced the Sales of Goods and Services Act 1982)

This Act identifies the contract, which takes place between the seller (therapist) and the customer (client), when a product is purchased. This Act makes the seller responsible for ensuring that the goods are of good merchantable quality. It covers all goods, even those used as part of the treatment. It requires that the person giving the service must do so with reasonable care and skill, within a reasonable time and for a reasonable charge.

Insurance

Employers Liability Act 1969

Employers must take out insurance policies in case of claims by employees for injury, disease or illness related to the workplace. It protects an employer against any claims made by an employee.

A certificate must be displayed at work to show that the employer has this insurance.

- Public liability insurance – this insurance protects you if a client or member of the public becomes injured on your premises.

- Product liability insurance – this type of insurance protects you against claims arising from products used by clients.

- Treatment liability insurance – this insurance protects you in the event of a claim arising from malpractice.

Write a brief description of the listed legislation, insurance and good practice. Should you need more writing space use a separate sheet of paper.

Legislation/guidelines   Brief description

Health and Safety at
Work Act 1974   _____

                  _____

Fire Precautions
Act 1971   _____

                  _____

COSHH 1999   _____

                  _____

Electricity at Work
Regulations 1990 _____

                  _____

RIDDOR 1995   _____

                  _____

First Aid Regulations
1981   _____

                  _____

Local Government
Act 1982   _____

                  _____

Codes of Practice _____

                  _____

Legislation/guidelines	Brief description
Code of Ethics	
Performing rights	
Data Protection Act 1998	
Consumer Protection Act 1987	
Trade Descriptions Acts 1968 and 1972	
Sales and Supply of Goods Act 1994	
Employers liability insurance (1969 Act)	
Public liability insurance	
Product liability insurance	
Treatment liability insurance	

Business plan

You may need to put together a business plan related to setting up an aromatherapy business. You will need to do some research on this subject. The following information will help you to prepare your business plan.

Research plan

- Research local competition. How much do they charge for treatments? What are their hours of business?

- Research the prices of products and equipment that you will need to start your business.

- How will you advertise and maintain public relations? How much will advertising your business cost?

- Carry out market research in the area where you propose to run your business. Are people interested in the services you have to offer?

- Will you be self-financed or will you require external finance, such as taking out a loan? Maybe seek the professional advice of an accountant.

- What insurance policies will you need to take out and how much will it cost?

- Research what is meant by the terms 'freehold' and 'leasehold'.

- Will you rent a room? How much will you pay?

- Will you run a mobile business? What costs are involved?

- Research all health, safety and hygiene issues and also cost these in if necessary.

- Consider the catchment area. Who are you trying to attract and from where?

- If you take over an existing business what improvement could you make?

> **Note**
>
> Banks will give you professional advice regarding setting up a business.

Treatment room

- What are the considerations when choosing a treatment room? Is there a place for clients to park? Will there be passing trade?

- What colour scheme will you have for your room?

- Draw a plan of your treatment room and consider all equipment and resources you will need.

Clients and services

- How will you ensure client satisfaction so that the client returns for future treatments?

- How much will you charge clients for each treatment? How long will each treatment take? You will need to ensure that the treatments are cost-effective.

- How will you ensure you maximise profitability, i.e. timekeeping, minimise wastage, etc?

- Will you require staff?

Note

It is a good idea to design a price list, and a leaflet, giving a brief outline of the services you will provide.

Write your answers to the questions below, then check against the sample answers on the web site (www.saloneducation.co.uk).

1. Why should you be aware of and follow all legislation relating to aromatherapy treatment?

2. Why is it important to take out relevant insurance policies when providing aromatherapy treatment?

3. How can a good business plan help ensure business success?

The following reference chart is useful for selecting essential oils to suit the needs of individual clients. For instance, if a client suffers with a skin condition such as eczema you can select a top, middle and base note to help with that condition. Chapter 5 discusses the essential oils in detail, including their properties and which oils blend well with each other to create a synergistic blend.

The key below shows different letters that represent ways of using the oils. For example, C stands for compress so it is recommended that a compress may be used for this condition.

M – *massage*

I – *inhalation*

C – *compress*

N – *neat*

B – *bath*

Table 9.1 Essential oils and conditions

Condition	Top note	Middle note	Base note
Circulatory			
High blood pressure (B, M – ensure doctor's advice is sought)	Lemon, clary sage, sweet orange	Lavender, melissa, marjoram	Neroli, ylang-ylang, valerian
Low blood pressure (B, M – ensure doctor's advice is sought)	Thyme	Peppermint, rosemary	
Piles (haemorrhoids) (B, M)	Lemon	Juniper, cypress, geranium	Myrrh, frankincense
Poor circulation (M, B)	Lemon, thyme, ginger, eucalyptus	Black pepper, pine, cypress, peppermint, rosemary	Benzoin, neroli, rose (cabbage or damask)
Varicose veins (B)	Lemon, orange	Cypress, lavender, rosemary, peppermint	Neroli
Digestive system			
Colic (B, M, C)	Bergamot, clary sage	Black pepper, melissa, fennel, peppermint, carrot seed, lavender, marjoram	Clove, ginger
Constipation and sluggish digestion (M, B, C)	Mandarin, orange	Black pepper, rosemary, fennel, marjoram	
Diarrhoea (M, B, C)	Eucalyptus	Chamomile (all types), lavender, peppermint, cypress	Clove, myrrh, sandalwood, ginger
Flatulence (M, B, C)	Bergamot, basil, mandarin, orange, petitgrain	Fennel, lavender, rosemary, peppermint	Ginger, myrrh
Indigestion (M, B)	Thyme, basil, bergamot, lemongrass, petitgrain, mandarin	Fennel, black pepper, chamomile (all types)	Clove

Table 9.1 (cont.)   Essential oils and conditions

Condition	Top note	Middle note	Base note
Irritable bowel syndrome (M, C, B)	Mandarin, petitgrain	Black pepper, marjoram, fennel rosemary peppermint, chamomile (Roman)	Ginger, neroli
Loss of appetite (I, M, B)	Bergamot	Black pepper, fennel, juniper	Ginger
Nausea/vomiting (I, M, B)	Basil, ginger	Fennel, melissa, peppermint, black pepper, chamomile (German and Roman)	Sandalwood, clove, ginger
Head			
Abscess (C, M, B)	Tea tree, thyme, lemon, eucalyptus	Lavender, chamomile, juniper	Sandalwood
Alopecia (loss of hair) (M, C, B)	Thyme, clary sage, lemon	Rosemary, carrot seed	Ylang-ylang
Conjunctivitis (M, B) (do not touch eyes)	Lemon	Lavender, chamomile (all types)	Rose (both types)
Dandruff (M, B)	Tea tree, lemongrass	Rosemary	Patchouli
Earache (M, B, C)	Basil	Lavender, chamomile (German and Roman)	
Oily hair (M, B)	Clary sage, lemon, petitgrain, grapefruit	Juniper, cypress	Frankincense, ylang-ylang, cedarwood, patchouli
Headache (M, B, C, I)	Clary sage, eucalyptus, thyme, grapefruit, lemongrass, basil, cajeput	Peppermint, lavender, rosemary, black pepper, chamomile, rosewood	Rose (both types), valerian
Head lice (B, M)	Tea tree, eucalyptus, thyme	Rosemary, geranium, lavender, pine	

Table 9.1 (cont.)   Essential oils and conditions

Condition	Top note	Middle note	Base note
Migraine (to help prevent) (M, B, C)	Basil, clary sage, lemongrass, eucalyptus	Melissa, rosemary peppermint, chamomile (German and Roman), lavender, marjoram	Valerian
Nosebleed (to help prevent) (I, M, B, C)	Lemon	Lavender, cypress	Rose (both types)
Sore throat (C, M, B)	Tea tree, thyme, cajeput, lemon, ginger, eucalyptus, bergamot	Geranium, lavender, pine	Myrrh, sandalwood
Toothache (C, M, B)	Cajeput	Black pepper, chamomile (all types), fennel lavender, peppermint, marjoram	Clove
Muscular and joints			
Aches and pains/ muscular tension (C, M, B)	Basil, eucalyptus, thyme	Black pepper, juniper, lavender, rosemary, pine, chamomile (German and Roman)	Vetiver
Arthritis/ rheumatism (C, M, B)	Eucalyptus, lemon, thyme, ginger	Chamomile (German and Roman), lavender, rosemary, marjoram, fennel	Benzoin, clove, vetiver
Cramp (C, M, B)	Basil, clary sage, thyme	Cypress, lavender, chamomile, (all types), marjoram, rosemary, pine	Jasmine, vetiver
Fibrositis/frozen shoulder (C, M, B)	Clary sage, ginger	Rosemary, lavender, peppermint, marjoram, black pepper	Clove, frankincense
Sprains and strains (C, B)	Eucalyptus, ginger, thyme	Lavender, rosemary, pine, chamomile, (German and Roman), black pepper	Clove, vetiver

Table 9.1 (cont.)   Essential oils and conditions

Condition	Top note	Middle note	Base note
Nervous			
Anxiety (M, B, I)	Thyme, basil, bergamot, clary sage, mandarin, sweet orange, tea tree, petitgrain	Chamomile (all types), cypress, pine, geranium, juniper, lavender, marjoram, melissa, rosewood	Cedarwood, frankincense, neroli, rose, valerian, vetiver, jasmine, patchouli, sandalwood, benzoin, ylang-ylang
Depression (M, B, I)	Bergamot, clary sage, lemongrass, basil, petitgrain, grapefruit	Lavender, chamomile (Maroc and German), marjoram, rosewood, geranium	Sandalwood, rose, ylang-ylang, patchouli, jasmine, neroli, frankincense, valerian
Insomnia (M, B, I)	Bergamot, basil, clary sage, mandarin, sweet orange, petitgrain	Juniper, geranium, lavender, marjoram, melissa, cypress, chamomile (all types)	Neroli, rose, sandalwood, frankincense, jasmine, ylang-ylang, valerian, vetiver
Mental fatigue (M, B, I)	Basil, thyme, clary sage, petitgrain, lemongrass, eucalyptus, ginger, grapefruit	Peppermint, rosemary, pine, lavender	Jasmine, vetiver, patchouli, ylang-ylang
Nervous tension and stress (M, I, B)	Clary sage, basil, bergamot, mandarin, orange, petitgrain	Lavender, lemongrass, melissa, peppermint, chamomile (all types), cypress, juniper, geranium, pine, rosewood	Benzoin, ylang-ylang, frankincense, vetiver, jasmine, valerian, patchouli
Poor memory (I, M, B)	Basil, thyme	Rosemary, peppermint, rosewood	
Shock (I, B)	Orange, clary, sage, mandarin	Melissa, geranium, lavender	Rose, valerian

Table 9.1 (cont.)   **Essential oils and conditions**

Condition	Top note	Middle note	Base note
Reproductive system			
Frigidity (M, I, B)	Clary sage	Rosewood	Jasmine, ginger, sandalwood, ylang-ylang, neroli, rose
Irregular periods (C, M, B)	Basil, clary sage	Lavender, fennel, melissa, chamomile (Roman and Maroc), peppermint, rosemary, juniper, marjoram, carrot seed	Rose, frankincense, myrrh, vetiver
Labour pain (C, M, B)	Clary sage	Lavender	Rose, jasmine, neroli
Lack of periods (amenorrhoea) (C, M, B)	Clary sage, basil	Chamomile (Roman and Maroc), fennel, melissa, carrot seed, marjoram, juniper	Rose, myrrh, vetiver
Menopausal problems (M, B)	Clary sage, bergamont	Cypress, fennel, geranium, chamomile (German and Roman)	Jasmine, rose, ylang-ylang, neroli
Period pain (dysmenorrhoea) (C, M, B)	Cajeput, basil, clary sage	Marjoram, melissa, cypress, chamomile (all types), juniper, rosemary, lavender, carrot seed, geranium	Rose, jasmine, frankincense
Pre-menstrual syndrome (PMS) (M, B, I)	Clary sage, bergamot	Geranium, lavender, chamomile (German and Maroc), melissa, marjoram, rosemary, rosewood, fennel, juniper	Rose, neroli, ylang-ylang

Table 9.1 (cont.) Essential oils and conditions

Condition	Top note	Middle note	Base note
Respiratory system			
Asthma (to help prevent) (M, B)	Mandarin, thyme, basil, cajeput, clary sage	Marjoram, melissa, cypress, lavender, peppermint, fennel	Clove, benzoin
Bronchitis (M, B)	Bergamot, basil, eucalyptus, cajeput, tea tree, thyme	Rosemary, pine, peppermint, lavender, cypress, melissa	Sandalwood, clove, benzoin, frankincense, myrrh
Catarrh (M, B)	Eucalyptus, thyme, lemon, tea tree	Black pepper, marjoram, lavender, peppermint	Frankincense, sandalwood, jasmine, myrrh
Colds/flu (to help prevent and treat) (M, B, I)	Eucalyptus, lemon, thyme, tea tree	Lavender, pine, peppermint, cypress	Sandalwood, benzoin, myrrh, frankincense
Coughs (M, B, I)	Eucalyptus, thyme, lemon, tea tree	Black pepper, lavender, cypress	Benzoin, jasmine, myrrh, frankincense
Skin			
Acne (M, B)	Lemongrass, clary sage, bergamot, tea tree, petitgrain, grapefruit	Chamomile (all types), lavender, juniper	Patchouli, clove, ylang-ylang
Athlete's foot (C, B)	Lemongrass, tea tree	Lavender, geranium	Patchouli, cedarwood, myrrh
Boils (C, B)	Thyme, lemon, clary sage, eucalyptus, tea tree	Chamomile (all types), lavender	Myrrh, cedarwood
Burns (C, B, N – lavender)	Eucalyptus, tea tree	Chamomile (German and Roman), geranium, lavender	Clove, patchouli
Cellulite (M, B)	Grapefruit, lemon, thyme	Juniper, fennel, cypress, rosemary	Patchouli, cedarwood, benzoin
Cold sores (B, N – tea tree)	Tea tree, lemon, eucalyptus, bergamot, thyme	Melissa, pine	Rose, clove

Table 9.1 (cont.) Essential oils and conditions

Condition	Top note	Middle note	Base note
Cuts, minor injuries (C, B, N – lavender)	Tea tree, eucalyptus, lemon	Lavender, geranium, chamomile (all types)	Benzoin, clove, vetiver
Dilated capillaries (M, B, C)	Lemon, thyme, grapefruit	Cypress, rosewood	Rose, frankincense
Dermatitis (C, M, B)	Thyme	Chamomile (German and Roman), lavender,geranium, juniper, peppermint, carrot seed	Patchouli, myrrh
Dry and sensitive skin (M, B)		Lavender, chamomile (all types), geranium, rosewood	Rose, neroli, jasmine, ylang-ylang, sandalwood, frankincense
Eczema (M, B)	Bergamot, thyme, tea tree	Chamomile (all types), geranium, lavender, juniper, carrot seed, melissa	Patchouli, rose, myrrh, sandalwood
Oily skin (M, B)	Lemon, bergamot, tea tree, petitgrain, clary sage, lemongrass	Geranium, lavender, cypress, juniper, rosemary, carrot seed	Ylang-ylang, sandalwood, patchouli, vetiver, cedarwood
Insect bites/stings (B, C, N – lavender)	Basil, bergamot, tea tree, cajeput, eucalyptus	Melissa, lavender, chamomile (all types), juniper	Ylang-ylang, benzoin, myrrh
Mature skin (M, B)	Clary sage	Lavender, melissa, rosemary, geranium	Neroli, jasmine, myrrh, frankincense, rose, benzoin
Psoriasis (M, B, I)	Bergamot, clary sage, thyme, tea tree	Lavender, carrot seed, chamomile (all types), geranium, juniper	Sandalwood, frankincense myrrh, rose
Ringworm (B, C)	Lemongrass, tea tree	Geranium, lavender	Myrrh, patchouli, cedarwood
Scars (M, B, C)	Mandarin	Carrot seed	Frankincense, sandalwood, patchouli, vetiver

Table 9.1 (cont.)   Essential oils and conditions

Condition	Top note	Middle note	Base note
Spots (M, B)	Tea tree, lemon, mandarin, basil, bergamot, cajeput, eucalyptus	Chamomile (all types), lavender	Sandalwood, patchouli, ylang-ylang
Stretch marks (M, B)	Mandarin	Lavender, rosewood	Frankincense, patchouli, neroli, sandalwood
Thrush (B, M)	Tea tree, lemongrass	Geranium	Myrrh
Warts/verruca (B, N – lemon or tea tree)	Bergamot, eucalyptus, lemon, tea tree	Melissa	Clove
Wounds (B, C, N – lavender, tea tree)	Tea tree, eucalyptus, bergamot, thyme	Chamomile (all types), lavender, geranium, rosemary, juniper	Frankincense, myrrh, benzoin, patchouli
Wrinkles (M, B)	Mandarin, orange	Rosemary, fennel, carrot seed, geranium	Frankincense, neroli, patchouli, rose, sandalwood, jasmine
Urinary			
Cystitis (B, M)	Bergamot, eucalyptus, cajeput, tea tree	Chamomile (German and Roman) fennel, lavender, pine, juniper	Sandalwood, frankincense, benzoin
Fluid retention (M, B)	Eucalyptus, grapefruit, lemon, mandarin	Fennel, juniper, rosemary, cypress, geranium, carrot seed	Patchouli, cedarwood
Others			
Relaxation (M, B, I)	Bergamot, clary sage	Geranium, rose, lavender, chamomile	Sandalwood, ylang-ylang, frankincense, jasmine, rose
Uplifting (M, B, I)	Bergamot, grapefruit	Lavender, rosemary	Neroli, valerian
Stimulating and motivating (M, B, I)	Bergamot, lemon, grapefruit	Lavender, cypress, rosemary, geranium	Ginger, neroli

Table 9.1 (cont.) Essential oils and conditions

Condition	Top note	Middle note	Base note
Insect repellent (M, B)	Lemongrass, bergamot, eucalyptus	Melissa, rosemary, cypress	Clove, patchouli, cedarwood
Obesity (M, B)	Lemon, mandarin, grapefruit	Fennel, juniper	Cedarwood, patchouli
Hangover (M, B)	Grapefruit	Lavender, rosemary, fennel, juniper	Sandalwood

Note

Other conditions and useful essential oils can be written in the empty boxes.

Examination Preparation

The following multiple choice questions will help you to prepare for aromatherapy examinations. Decide the correct answer and put a circle around either a, b, c or d.

1. What kind of treatment do we give when we take into account the mind, body and spirit to improve the health of an individual?

    (a) spiritualistic   (c) individualistic

    (b) holistic   (d) specialistic

2. While working in a laboratory, who found that a burnt hand healed quickly when plunged into lavender oil?

    (a) Gattefosse   (c) Madame Maury

    (b) Dr Jean Valnet   (d) Hippocrates

3. Which of the following is *not* a possible skin reaction to essential oils?

    (a) phototoxicity   (c) sensitisation

    (b) irritation   (d) carotoxicity

4. What percentage of patient visits to the doctor are thought to be stress-related?

   (a) 20%   (c) 60%

   (b) 40%   (d) 90%

5. When storing essential oils ensure that:

   (a) the oils are stored in dark amber bottles in a cool, dark place

   (b) the oils are stored in clear bottles in a fridge

   (c) the oils are stored in dark amber bottles in direct sunlight

   (d) the oils are stored in clear bottles near a source of heat

6. With the exception of citrus oils essential oils will generally last for about how long?

   (a) 1 year   (c) 3 years

   (b) 2 years   (d) 4 years

7. Which of the following essential oils should *not* be used at all?

   (a) patchouli   (c) ylang-ylang

   (b) tansy   (d) rosewood

8. Essential oils will *not* dissolve in:

   (a) full–fat milk   (c) water

   (b) alcohol   (d) vegetable oil

9. Which of the following essential oils can be applied neat to the skin?

    (a) peppermint   (c) bergamot

    (b) cedarwood   (d) lavender

10. When blending essential and carrier oils you should ensure a dilution of what percentage?

    (a) 2%   (c) 4%

    (b) 3%   (d) 5%

11. Essential oils regarded as top notes are mostly obtained from:

    (a) flowers   (c) resins

    (b) herbs   (d) fruits

12. When essential oils are mixed together and enhance each other's properties they are said to make:

    (a) a synergistic blend   (c) an amicable blend

    (b) a complementary blend   (d) an enhancing blend

13. Which of the following is *not* a type of carrier oil used in aromatherapy?

    (a) grapeseed   (c) sweet almond

    (b) wheatgerm   (d) grass-seed

14. Which of the following is *not* a common type of hydrolat?

   (a) lavender water
   (c) jojoba water
   (b) tea tree water
   (d) rose water

15. Which of the following is *not* an example of an essential oil extraction method?

   (a) expression
   (c) solvent extraction
   (b) compression
   (d) steam distillation

16. An essential oil that has emmenagogue properties will:

   (a) help bring on menstruation
   (c) aid digestion of food
   (b) help to reduce fevers
   (d) help to destroy fungi

17. Which of the following is *not* a type of chemical found in essential oils?

   (a) ketones
   (c) teroxides
   (b) aldehydes
   (d) terpenes

18. The Latin name for black pepper is:

   (a) *Cananga odorata*
   (c) *Piper nigrum*
   (b) *Ocimum basilicum*
   (d) *Lavendula angustofolia*

19. Which of the following is *not* a type of botanical family?

   (a) Labitae
   (c) Rutaceae
   (b) Planteceae
   (d) Compositae

20. Which of the following is *not* a type of basil?

    (a) exotic   (c) French

    (b) eugenol   (d) Italian

21. Which essential oil is found in Earl Grey tea?

    (a) bergamot   (c) rose

    (b) geranium   (d) petitgrain

22. Chamazulene gives this oil its deep blue colour:

    (a) chamomile Maroc   (c) thyme

    (b) chamomile German   (d) frankincense

23. Which of the following essential oils are extracted from daisy-like flowers?

    (a) benzoin   (c) chamomile Roman

    (b) neroli   (d) ginger

24. If swallowed, this essential oil can be fatal:

    (a) petitgrain   (c) grapefruit

    (b) eucalyptus   (d) ylang-ylang

25. This essential oil is also known as olibanum:

    (a) cajeput   (c) frankincense

    (b) carrot seed   (d) jasmine

26. This essential oil is often added to cakes and biscuits as it is good for the digestive system:

    (a) ginger   (c) clary sage
    (b) rosewood   (d) myrrh

27. Berries from this plant are used in the production of gin:

    (a) clove   (c) juniper
    (b) black pepper   (d) marjoram

28. This plant is often used to flavour toothpaste, confectionery and in medicine:

    (a) vetiver   (c) peppermint
    (b) ylang-ylang   (d) patchouli

29. Rosa centifolia is also known as:

    (a) rose, lettuce   (c) rose, carrot
    (b) rose, cabbage   (d) rose, sprouts

30. Rosmarinus officinalis is the Latin name for which plant?

    (a) rose, damask   (c) rosemary
    (b) rosewood   (d) thyme

31. These trees are protected in India and only cut down when mature:

    (a) cedarwood   (c) rosewood
    (b) lemon   (d) sandalwood

32. Bois de rose is also known as:

    (a) rosemary   (c) melissa

    (b) rosewood   (d) jasmine

33. This essential oil has antiviral, antibacterial and antifungal properties:

    (a) geranium   (c) black pepper

    (b) tea tree   (d) carrot seed

34. This essential oil is a well-known aphrodisiac:

    (a) patchouli   (c) ylang-ylang

    (b) grapefruit   (d) cedarwood

35. What term is used to define any medical reasons why aromatherapy treatment may not be carried out?

    (a) contra-indication   (c) contra-reason

    (b) contra-sign   (d) contra-action

36. Which of the following is not aftercare advice given after aromatherapy treatment?

    (a) do not bath/shower for twenty-four hours

    (b) drink plenty of water or herbal teas

    (c) do some vigorous exercise

    (d) avoid drinks containing caffeine

37. Effleurage is a French word meaning:

   (a) stroking

   (b) clapping

   (c) rubbing

   (d) pressing

38. Petrissage is a French word meaning:

   (a) cupping

   (b) kneading

   (c) wringing

   (d) patting

39. For what do the initials COSHH stand for?

   (a) control of substances hurtful to health

   (b) control of substances helpful to health

   (c) control of situations hazardous to health

   (d) control of substances hazardous to health

40. Which of the following types of legislation relates directly to employers and employees maintaining high standards of health and safety?

   (a) Consumer Protection Act 1987

   (b) RIDDOR

   (c) Data Protection Act 1998

   (d) Health and Safety at Work Act 1974

1. (b)	11. (d)	21. (a)	31. (d)
2. (a)	12. (a)	22. (b)	32. (b)
3. (d)	13. (d)	23. (c)	33. (b)
4. (c)	14. (c)	24. (b)	34. (c)
5. (a)	15. (b)	25. (c)	35. (a)
6. (b)	16. (a)	26. (a)	36. (c)
7. (b)	17. (c)	27. (c)	37. (a)
8. (c)	18. (c)	28. (c)	38. (b)
9. (d)	19. (b)	29. (b)	39. (d)
10. (a)	20 (d)	30. (c)	40. (d)

Index

Note: Page reference in italics indicate figures.

kaolin clay masks 36
ketones 65, 67
kneading (massage technique)
    198

labour pains 237
lavender 20, 31, 76, 124–5
lavender water 58
LBP (low blood pressure) 180,
    233
legislation 218–26
lemon 20, 28, 126–7
lemon balm (melissa) 134–5
lemongrass 128–9
limbic system 30
lime 17
Local Government
    (Miscellaneous Provisions) Act
    1982 223
low blood pressure (LBP) 180,
    233
lungs *30*
    and essential oil absorption
    29
lymphatic drainage massage 201
lymphatic system, effects of
    essential oils on 74–5

macadamia oil 48–9
maceration 45
magnesium carbonate clay masks
    36
mandarin 20, 130–1
marigold oil
    calendula (pot marigold)
        45–6
    tagetes 17, 46
marjoram, sweet 132–3
Maroc chamomile 98–9

masks, skin cleansing 35–6
massage treatment 28
    aftercare advice 189–90
    blends for client's home use
        192
    client preparation 171
    consultation 173–6
    contra-actions 191–2
    contraindications 177–82,
        184
    length of treatment session
        173
    massage movements and
        their effects 196–201
    referrals 185–6
    therapists 170–1
    therapy rooms 172
    treatment plans 187–89
mature skin type 34, 239
Maury, Mme Marguerite 4
Medieval times 3, *3*
meditation 210
    breathing exercise 209–10
melissa 133–4
memory, poor 236
menopausal problems 237
menstruation
    and aromatherapy treatment
        182
    emmanagogic oils and 20
    essential oils for conditions
        of 236
mental fatigue 236
meridians of the body 203, *203*,
    207
middle notes 38, 39
migraine 235
mineral oils 43
moisturisers, skin 35

molecules 65
monoterpenes 66
mugwort (armoise) 14
muscular system
    effects of essential oils on 75
    essential oils for conditions
        of 235
music 224
mustard 14
myrrh 135–6

nail diseases 181
nausea 234
negative stress 7, 9
neroli 20, 137–8
neroli water 58
nervous system *200*
    dysfunction of 180
    effects of essential oils on
        75–6
    essential oils for conditions
        of 236
neuromuscular massage 199–200
normal skin type 32
nosebleeds 235
notes of odours 38–9
nutmeg 18

obesity 242
odours, categorising 38–9
oedema (fluid retention) 74, 201,
    240
oestrogen stimulants 21, 77
oils *see* carrier oils; essential oils
oily skin type 33, 239
olfactory system 30, *30*
olibanum (frankincense) 20,
    112–13
olive oil 49

sunflower oil 52
sweet almond oil 42, 43–4
sweet fennel 110–11
sweet marjoram 132–3
sweet orange 17, 20, 140–1
sweet thyme 162
synergy 39–40

tagetes 17, 46
tansy 14
Taxol 5
tea tree 160–1
tea tree water 58
terpenes 65, 66
therapeutic properties of
   essential oils 70–2
therapists 170
   posture 171
therapy rooms 172, 230

thrombosis 180
thrush 240
thuja 14, 18
thyme
   red 162–3
   sweet 162
ti tree 160–1
toners, skin 35, 58
toothache 236
top notes 38, 39
toxicity 17–18
Trades Descriptions Acts 1968
   and 1972 225
treatment see massage treatment

urinary system
      effects of essential oils on 77
      essential oils for conditions
         of 240

valerian 164–5
Valnet, Dr Jean 4
vaporisers 27
varicose veins 181, 233
verrucas 240
vetiver 166–7
visualisation 211–12
vomiting 234

warts 240
wheatgerm oil 52–3
wintergreen 14, 18
wormseed 14, 18
wormwood 14, 18
wounds 240
wrinkles 240

ylang-ylang 20, 168–9